Tales from the

COLD
WAR

The U.S. Army in West Germany
1960-1975

Michael D. Mahler

UNG
UNIVERSITY *of*
NORTH GEORGIA™
UNIVERSITY PRESS

Published by:
University of North Georgia Press
Dahlonega, Georgia

Printing Support by:
Lightning Source Inc.
La Vergne, Tennessee

Cover and book design by Corey Parson.

ISBN: 978-1-940771-92-2

Printed in the United States of America

For more information, please visit: http://ung.edu/university-press
Or e-mail: ungpress@ung.edu

UNIVERSITY *of*
NORTH GEORGIA™
UNIVERSITY PRESS

Blue Ridge | Cumming | Dahlonega | Gainesville | Oconee

DEDICATION

To the ladies who come up in June,
We'll bid a fond adieu,
Here's hoping they be married soon,
And join the Army too.

From "Army Blue," a traditional West Point song

These tales of the Cold War army in the West Germany of the 1960s and '70s are dedicated to the Army wives of that era, and most especially to the ladies who came up in June 1958 to the U.S. Military Academy at West Point and joined the Army too by marrying members of my class. Army wives kept the families together during the long months when their husbands were in the field on training exercises and maneuvers preparing for an eventuality that thankfully never came to pass. In addition, they kept the social fabric of that Army strong by voluntarily running the Army Community Service and child care facilities on hundreds of small Army posts and by making sure that the junior enlisted wives who did not live in Army family housing could get to those posts to do their necessary shopping for essentials when their husbands were frequently gone for extended periods of time for field training. As their husbands were promoted and became field grade officers and commanders of those small posts spread across West Germany, they were frequently the authority of last resort when some young rear detachment commander was unsure what to do at 2 a.m. with the unit and their commander husbands gone to the field. They were a sisterhood of the strong and the independent without ever sacrificing the charm and the elegance with which they came to the life their husbands had chosen. Some of that group who dated members of my class and then married into our class are still with us today, thank God, and still keeping our stories from becoming too exaggerated.

I have written the tale of our life
For a sheltered people's mirth,
In jesting guise—but ye are wise,
And ye know what the jest is worth.

"Prelude" to *Department Ditties*
Rudyard Kipling, 1885

TABLE OF CONTENTS

INTRODUCTION

This is the story of life in the U.S. Army that was stationed in West Germany during the Cold War years, as seen by an officer who lived it in its armor units and its headquarters. During the Cold War, the U.S. Army had elements stationed around the world to face the potential Communist threat. Though a substantial force was stationed in Korea, the major instrument of deterrence was the U.S. Army Europe stationed in West Germany and called USAREUR by all who were connected with it. Headquartered in Heidelberg, Germany, its ground combat component was the Seventh Army, headquartered in Stuttgart until it was combined with the USAREUR headquarters in Heidelberg. Its Corps, Division, and border Armored Cavalry Regiments were spread out across West Germany in some 150 *kasernes* (garrisons), small two- or three-battalion posts with their own family quarters, small post exchange, small commissary (the Army's grocery stores), and a rudimentary medical clinic. The soldiers and their families living on these *kasernes* had a lot in common with those who lived in the small, isolated garrisons of the western frontier army of the United States in the 1800s.

There has been a good bit written, both fact and fiction, about that earlier frontier army and the Regular Army soldiers who manned those remote garrisons before the western frontier passed into history. USAREUR and Seventh Army has now transitioned into a deployable Seventh Army at a reduced strength of about 30,000 soldiers who are clustered at several large, recently expanded and modernized, hub installations in Germany and Italy. It is past time to tell the story of life in that 190,000-man force that fought the Cold War in West Germany. The soldiers and officers of that era are long gone from active service, and their story will soon pass from the collective memory. Here is one soldier's tale of life in that Army, which still had strong links to the horse cavalry of the pre-World War II Army and whose senior leaders were products of that war.

The senior leaders in USAREUR back then were all veterans of World War II, and their experiences influenced daily life. Many of the senior armor officers had joined the horse cavalry when they were commissioned in the late 1930s. They had made the transition from horse to armored vehicle at the beginning of World War II, but some still retained their enthusiasm for the horse by staying involved in the Olympic-level equestrian world or engaging in fox hunting in their spare time. On occasion, a horse could still be seen tethered to the railing of the post commander's quarters at Grafenwoehr, a major training area, at lunchtime in the early 1960s.

Many in the ranks of captain and above had served in the last days of World War II, and many of those captains had then been recalled to active duty for Korea. That recall had added sufficient years of service to their records to decide them on staying in until they could achieve retirement at the 20-year point of service, which was not so very far away. A lot of these captains never did get promoted to major, but they knew their armored vehicles, their maintenance, and their tank gunnery. And, of course, armor tactics were second nature to them. That expertise was equally true of the field grade officers. I well remember my first Army training test at the training area at Grafenwoehr in which our tank battalion opposed a mechanized infantry battalion. The opposing battalion was commanded by a fast-promotion lieutenant colonel destined to be a three-star general. He was ably supported by his dual-hatted operations officer and executive officer, who was a fast-promotion major destined to be a two-star general. Our older World War II veteran battalion commander literally ran tactical circles around the other battalion.

Many of the older captains were hard drinkers who had not put very much distance between themselves and their previous World War II combat experience. One of my first company commanders, a captain, habitually dove into a ditch every time the newly-minted West German air force flew over our columns in support of our field exercises. The German air force was on our side now, but it retained the wing markings from the earlier period, and the captain—who had developed the reflex during World War II—had some trouble shaking it.

My first division commander in the 4th Armored Division in Europe was General John K. Waters, the son-in-law of the World War II General George Patton. Waters had been captured in North Africa and was a major reason for Patton's later ill-fated tank task force being sent to rescue the American prisoners of war held at Hammelburg, Germany, as the Allied advance approached. World War II was still very close in memory to us in those days.

The links between the armored forces of the Cold War and the horse cavalry of the pre-World War II period were equally strong. When I reported to my first unit at Fort Knox, Kentucky, in 1959 as a 2nd Lieutenant prior to being assigned to West Germany for the first time, my first platoon sergeant in the 6th Armored Cavalry Regiment had enlisted in the horse cavalry just before World War II. General Creighton Abrams—the great armor leader of the Battle of the Bulge and, later, the Chief of Staff of the Army after his tour as the commander in Vietnam—shared a story with my Armor School officer class about the horse cavalry anti-tank tactics in his horse cavalry regiment pre-World War II. The general told us that the cavalry doctrine at that time was to form fours, circle the tank on horseback, and shoot at the tank's vision blocks with their pistols. By the 1960s, the horse was gone and we were well past shooting at tanks with pistols, but the memories of the doctrine was not that distant.

My regimental commander in the 6th Armored Cavalry was Colonel Tracy B. Harrington. He also had been commissioned into the horse cavalry in 1938 and had served in horse cavalry until 1940. He then transitioned into the armored cavalry units of World War II, which were called reconnaissance squadrons until some years after the war ended.

For most of its Cold War history, USAEUR and Seventh Army's ground combat formations consisted of two Armored Divisions, two Mechanized Infantry Divisions, and two or three Armored Cavalry Regiments, which patrolled the border between East and West Germany. These units were divided into two corps under the Seventh Army, which eventually was combined with the USAREUR headquarters in Heidelberg for economy's sake. V Corps was headquartered in Frankfurt, and VII Corps was headquartered just outside of Stuttgart.

In the years between the Korean War and the Vietnam War, draftee soldiers and Regular Army noncommissioned officers manned the armor units in which I served. These noncommissioned officers tended to rotate back and forth between armor units in Germany and Fort Hood or Fort Knox in the United States—with maybe an odd 13-month unaccompanied tour in Korea interrupting that cycle. The result was a close-knit, very professional noncommissioned officer corps.

The soldiers who manned these units, and the family members who accompanied the officers, noncommissioned officers, and some junior enlisted soldiers, lived on 150 installations and in ninety-five family housing areas. Fifty-one maintenance facilities and depots, ten hospitals, and five major training areas supported these folks. Some of these facilities were collocated, and some additional detachments guarding the West German nuclear capability lived in West German facilities. Additionally, large numbers of family members of junior enlisted soldiers–some authorized by the command and some not–lived "on the economy" in rented German apartments because Army family quarters were either not available or they were not eligible for them.

I was destined for this stage when I joined the 6th Armored Cavalry Regiment at Fort Knox, Kentucky, in early 1959. The regiment was scheduled to ship to Europe as a "Gyroscope" unit, which meant that its soldiers and family members as an entity would swap places with the 11th Armored Cavalry Regiment. They were then located in southern West Germany at Regensburg, Straubing, and Landshut manning the southern sector of the border facing Czechoslovakia. Our noncommissioned officers had largely come to the 6th Armored Cavalry from border duty with the 11th Armored Cavalry and were a tight-knit group, many of whom had served in the storied Constabulary forces of the West German occupation, which had only ended in 1956.

The Constabulary had been the main occupation force in West Germany from 1946 to 1952. They were known as the Circle C Cowboys because of their distinctive shoulder patch consisting of a large blue "C" centered on a blue-bordered circular yellow background with a diagonal red lightning bolt crossing the "C". It was a lightly-armored, highly-mobile force equipped with light tanks, armored cars, and machine gun-mounted jeeps and trucks. After the 1948 Berlin Blockade, it had started to transition into a heavier combat force as it became apparent that the West was going to be in a face-off with the Communist forces of Eastern Europe. By 1952, the Constabulary had been replaced by Regular Army units. The transition of the border Constabulary units into the border Armored Cavalry Regiments had taken place at about that time, and my noncommissioned officers loved to tell the story of the tank that had been buried in a field near the border because the newly-minted Armored Cavalry Regiment was about to end up with one more tank than it was authorized as part of the transition. If true, some farmer will no doubt be amazed one day to discover this souvenir of another era buried in their farm field somewhere between Straubing and Landshut, on the border between Germany and Czechoslovakia. Obviously, our inventory methods were a little less rigorous back then.

1

FIRST STATION

Dressed in the tan, tropical, worsted summer uniform of the period, with shirt, tie, and blouse (the official name for the uniform coat), I reported to the adjutant at the headquarters of the 6th Armored Cavalry Regiment at Fort Knox, Kentucky. The regiment was run in a very traditional manner under Colonel Tracy B. Harrington and the traditional way of reporting in on my first duty day influenced my coffee drinking habits ever after.

The colonel would see me after a bit, the adjutant told me, *Would I like a cup of coffee?* As a brand-new 2nd lieutenant, I was not about to say no to anything offered by a senior 1st lieutenant. As I finished my first cup of coffee, I was ushered into the regimental commander's office, where I was politely offered a cup of coffee while I had my interview. I was then directed to the battalion headquarters of the 3rd Battalion to which I was to be assigned. I again reported to the adjutant and was again offered a cup of coffee until the battalion commander was free. When I went in to see my new battalion commander, I was offered still another cup of coffee.

After being given my company assignment, I reported in to the orderly room of G Company, where I was told the company commander was in the mess hall. I joined him there and had another cup of coffee while we got acquainted. The noon meal was not far away by then, and I had still another cup of coffee with the meal as I met my fellow platoon leaders. By noon, I was on a coffee high with a rumbling stomach to match. That cured me! I never drank coffee between meals again, though I was to be surrounded by folks who always had a mug of lukewarm coffee close at hand.

Shortly after I joined the regiment, I was informed that I would make my formal call on the regimental commander and his wife on a designated evening. This was the then-traditional 10-minute visit—the length of one cigarette—to the commanding officer and his wife that each new officer and spouse made so that the respective couples could identify and get an impression of each other. In this case, it was a "mass call" evening during which a number of new lieutenants and their spouses were rotated in and out of the colonel's quarters on an overlapping schedule. Brand new to the army and not having worn our blue dress uniforms very much, getting there on time and with a properly rigged out dress uniform caused us a certain amount of anxiety.

I made my preparations and arrived at the colonel's door exactly on time, just as another couple scheduled for the same time arrived. As the door opened to our knock, I noticed that the other lieutenant had forgotten to attach his branch and "U.S." insignia to the appropriate spots on the lapels of his blue uniform. There was no time to say anything—and the problem of what to do, given the time schedule allotted for each caller would have presented still another dilemma. I hoped for the lieutenant's sake that nobody would notice his missing brass, but about five minutes into the call, Mrs. Harrington, intent on making small talk, asked the lieutenant what his branch of service was since she could not tell from his blue uniform blouse. At that moment he became aware of his uniform problem, though he answered the question quickly enough. Such were the rites of passage for we young officers as we learned our way around the many and varied challenges of our new careers.

My first platoon had a scout section of four machine gun mounted jeeps; an infantry squad that rode in an M59 (the hulking, two-engine predecessor to the M113 armored personnel carrier); an 81mm mortar carried in a three-quarter ton truck and trailer; and a tank section of three 25-ton M41 Walker Bulldog tanks, which mounted a 76mm main gun system that was partially manual and partially electric-hydraulic and had an optical range finder and sights. The 81mm mortar was eliminated from armor units a short time later in favor of a track-mounted (modified M59's or M113's) 4.2 inch mortar. The mostly Spanish-speaking mortar men could assemble and bring that 81mm mortar—carried dismantled in the truck bed—into action faster than the later fully-assembled, track-mounted weapon with all its specially adapted fittings could be made ready to fire. The platoon leader also had a jeep, and the doctrine was that he would replace the platoon sergeant in his M41 tank and the sergeant would switch to the jeep upon contact with the enemy.

I had a core of very professional noncommissioned officers as the cadre and a skeleton crew for most of my vehicles, though the mortar squad was at full strength. The 6th Armored Cavalry Regiment was to be brought up to full strength with draftee recruits, and this cadre would then train them up to deployment readiness standards. The entire unit, with accompanying families, would then ship over to West Germany under what was known as Operation Gyroscope: a unit rotation in which the entire unit traded places with a similar unit in West Germany, the 11th Armored Cavalry Regiment, in this instance. That was the understanding when I left Fort Knox to marry my fiancée at West Point in June of 1959. My wife and I were married at West Point and spent our wedding night in New York City. The next morning we flew to Louisville, Kentucky, believing that our honeymoon would be on the ship which carried the 6th Armored Cavalry Regiment to its new assignment in Europe. We returned from our wedding to find that Operation Gyroscope had been cancelled—along with our projected honeymoon.

We settled in at Fort Knox, where I continued to train the recruits that the regiment had acquired, while my wife and I waited for individual assignment orders to U.S. Army Europe. Though it was permissible for my wife to share my bachelor officer quarters for a short time on a temporary basis, we needed to find a place to live. Junior officers were placed on a very long waiting list for quarters on post, though some additional quarters were under construction. Consequently, we ventured out into rural Kentucky to see what $222.30 a month, plus a quarters allowance of $85.50 a month, would get us. I have never been quite sure how or why our marriage survived for more than 50 years after that first house-hunting experience.

We were shown structures that looked a lot like chicken coops, some of which you could actually see the ground through the floor. Most had running water and some kind of kitchen and bathroom facility, but they were all pretty primitive. We finally located an apartment in a two-story building in the little town of West Point, Kentucky, a few miles from the post. The building had two apartments on each of the two floors, with a shared bathroom between them on each floor. The apartments consisted of a bedroom/living room and a kitchen. Unfortunately, the owner had suffered a heart attack while he was constructing the apartment building next to his home, so it had stood open to the Kentucky weather for over a year. The result was all the doorframes and window frames in the building were warped out of plumb and the floors waved a bit. Nevertheless, the apartments were off the ground and had the necessary plumbing. The bonus was that the owner's house next door had a framed bullet by its front door, a memento of General Forrest's foray north during the Civil War.

We moved into the apartment with our meager start-up household goods. The first morning, the alarm went off very early so my wife could drive me on to Fort Knox in time to be at my company for the first formation of the day. I jumped out of bed and into my laid-out, starched fatigue uniform. I finished lacing my boots and blousing my fatigue trousers over them then turned around to find my new wife sitting on the edge of the bed fully dressed but half asleep, and clearly wondering what was the emergency the alarm clock had seemed to indicate. And so we started our army life together.

Fortunately, some family quarters that were under construction came on line in a month or so, and we gladly moved into them. These brick fourplexes came with a dining room, living room, modern kitchen, and three bedrooms. Now our problem was having no furniture except for a bed that we had purchased, a couple of folding lawn chairs, and an end table from my wife's college dorm room. But the Army understood about junior officers and their pay—sort of. The post quartermaster supplied a wood dining room set, the replicas of which we were to live with for the next 25 years in various quarters in Europe. My troop supply room also gladly signed out to me a steel army cot, four mattresses, and two pillows. We folded two mattresses each in half lengthwise to form cushions on the cot, rolled two mattresses together lengthwise and tied to work as a backrest against the wall, and wrapped the pillows around the cot railings at the head and foot. With some cheap material and my wife's sewing machine, we had a sofa, even if it was a little high off the floor so that most users were left with dangling feet. The material showed up as curtains in a number of sets of quarters in the following years, and for a time, even provided a bathrobe for my wife. Thank God she could sew.

These newly-constructed quarters were so new that they had no landscaping, so the red clay earth of Kentucky was their backdrop–dusty in dry, windy weather and muddy in wet weather. In fact, the back yards sloped down to a large drainage ditch between the rows of quarters to carry the runoff from the common heavy downpours. Each set of quarters had a tiny concrete pad and a storage shed attached in the back. In wet weather, you ventured off the pad at your risk. Shortly after we moved in and manufactured our living room furniture, my mother visited us, checking up on the newlyweds. She had put some items out to dry on the issue umbrella-style clothesline, which served two sets of quarters and was set in what some day would be the backyard, when it started to pour. In an attempt to rescue the drying items, she ran out to the clothesline and got stuck in the red earthen gumbo. We rescued her, the no longer drying clothes, and her shoes separately—the latter two only after the ground dried out sufficiently to support us.

Meanwhile, the regiment had its recruits, and they had to be trained despite the cancellation of Operation Gyroscope. We became a basic training organization doing all the training that the Training Center, across post, did for the bulk of new Army recruits. It was pretty routine duty, except for an unusual uniform incident that surpassed that lieutenant's lack of brass on his blues by a whole lot.

For some reason, the Army had introduced a summer uniform for certain climate conditions consisting of a short-sleeved shirt, shorts that came to just above the knee, and knee socks. The uniforms were cotton and so heavily starched, in keeping with the practice of the day, that whatever ventilation value was gained from the short sleeves and shorts was lost in the practically impervious wall of starch. Summer temperatures at Fort Knox qualified for this uniform, and there was the inevitable Saturday morning inspection for the entire regiment to ensure that everybody had all the pieces of the uniform and knew how to wear them. On the appointed morning, we all turned out. I, however, was one recruit short in my platoon. When the other recruits were questioned, my platoon sergeant and I were told that he was in the barracks but would not come out to formation. We hustled into the barracks and found our recruit in a very embarrassing position. He was so well endowed that his equipment fell below the bottom hem of his shorts. We excused him from formation. I don't remember ever wearing that uniform again.

In the fall of 1959, my orders to USAREUR finally came through. I was to be assigned to the 1st Medium Tank Battalion, 37th Armor (1-37th Armor) in the 4th Armored Division at a little two-battalion post located at Crailsheim, West Germany. The next challenge was concurrent travel! The Army would not let your family travel with you unless quarters were available at your assigned post in West Germany. Of course, there were never enough quarters for those assigned to these small posts, and there was a long waiting list for quarters where we were assigned. However, we found a loophole. If you had family in Europe who would vouch that they had a place for your wife, you could get concurrent travel. Conveniently, my wife had an uncle living in Italy, and they were glad to offer us in writing a place to live. That written word was sufficient, though we never even visited them in Italy. And so, in February of 1960, we set out for Germany in a four-engine Constellation. Rhein Main Air Force Base, just outside of Frankfurt, West Germany, was our destination.

2

SETTLING IN

We had a long but uneventful flight from the United States to West Germany, complete with a stop in Shannon, Ireland, where we purchased a piece of jewelry in the duty-free shop. It was the first piece of jewelry I had ever purchased for my wife, aside from her wedding gift, and she wore it for the next 5o years. We landed at Rhein Main Air Force Base just outside of Frankfurt and site of the current Frankfurt International Airport. It was the bustling hub through which most Army members and their families processed into USAREUR. We were processed quickly, stayed the night in the transient quarters on the base, and traveled to Crailsheim the next day.

Crailsheim is a small town on the Jagst River, centrally isolated midway between Stuttgart and Nuremberg on Highway 14, which at that time was a curvy, two-lane asphalt road. Much later it became a modern *autobahn*. Crailsheim had been a highway and rail junction during World War II and had been largely destroyed by tank and artillery fire. So, of course, we had stationed a tank battalion and an artillery battalion at the nearby Army post, called a *kaserne* in German. Stone flak towers still overlooked the city, decorating the low hills and rolling farm fields surrounding it. Antiaircraft artillery guns had been placed atop these silo-like structures to improve the defense against Allied air attacks. The city had largely been rebuilt by the time we arrived, and I never detected any resentment about the composition of the units stationed nearby.

Almost every German town has a "Post Hotel," the genesis being that the post coaches used to stop there. We were taken to our Post Hotel, where we moved in to a third-floor room (no elevator, of course) under the gables. The hotel was centrally located in the small city and had a dining room where we could get breakfast and dinner. My sponsor was kind enough to provide transportation back and forth to the post, which was a couple of miles back down Highway 14 toward Stuttgart. I came back from my first duty day, a raw typical German winter day, to find my wife sitting huddled on top of the radiator in her winter coat trying to stay warm. The hotel did not like to waste heat during the day!

The West German government at this time was concerned about refugees from East Germany having places to live after they fled west. This concern translated into a subsidy if a homeowner included a rental apartment in the house that he was building, but there was no restriction as to whom that apartment could be rented. That subsidy meant that many newer homes had rental apartments, and that enabled us to find an apartment on the outskirts of town in a neighborhood of fairly new single-family homes. Once again, we were on the second floor and once again our apartment consisted of two rooms: a living room with a fold out sofa and a kitchen. The hot water for the kitchen came from a wall tank over the bathtub in the bathroom down the hall, which we shared with the grandmother of the house. Heating came from a little iron potbellied stove, the coal bricks for which we brought up from the basement in a rather ornate coal scuttle. It was comfortable, but it took a lot of duct tape to keep the cold, wet air from coming through the large window in front of the kitchen table where we spent a lot of time.

The next order of business was a USAREUR private vehicle driver's license. The challenge here were the pages of German road signs that had to be memorized. The written part of the test and the road-sign recognition part were administered together, and very few mistakes were allowed for a passing grade. Though some of the signs have since crept into usage in the United States, they were all strange to us at the time. Our lack of fluency in German meant that even the abbreviations on some of the sign faces were of very little help. As an aside, more than one newly-licensed American thought that *Einbahnstrasse* (one-way street) was actually the name of the street. After studying the rules of the road and the pages of signs for a week or so, my wife and I caught a ride to Dolan Barracks, the administrative headquarters for our support area a half hour's drive away at Schwabisch Hall. Miraculously we passed the test on the first try and were awarded our licenses.

We also discovered an Army swimming pool on that trip to Schwabisch Hall. Dolan Barracks had been a *Luftwaffe* air base during World War II and had all the amenities so dear to the flying arm. The swimming pool had survived the war and became a neat destination for us the following summer on the few hot weekends that occurred.

About the time that we earned our USAREUR driver's licenses, we received notification that our car—which we had turned in at the old Brooklyn Navy Yard just across the river from New York City for shipment at government expense—had arrived in Bremerhaven in northern Germany. The first time I could get free, I asked for and received a pass to go by train to pick up our car and drive back to Crailsheim. Despite our limited German, we made the train arrangements and traveled north. Somewhere around Frankfurt, we ended up in a compartment with a salesman from East Germany, who spent the rest of the trip giving us our first German lesson. Interestingly, at the time, well before the Berlin Wall went up, there was relatively free movement of people, goods, and trucks between East and West Germany, though a lot of paperwork was required to transit either way. That would all change in August 1961.

Late in the day, we pulled into Bremerhaven and got off amid a noisy crowd of *fussball* fans singing very strident drinking songs that sounded eerily like what the Hitler youth had been portrayed as singing during the Nazi era. Our newfound East German friend assured us that it was only a *fussball* team that was being exhorted. We said our goodbyes and found our way to the port and the transient quarters that were available for people claiming their cars. Fortunately, our 1954 Ford convertible arrived in good shape. The horror stories about cars that had been damaged or accidentally dropped during unloading were too numerous to be taken lightly until we were actually driving out the gate of the Army port.

We had plotted our route back to Crailsheim through Fulda, the headquarters of the 14th Armored Cavalry Regiment and one of its organic cavalry squadrons, because a couple whom we were very friendly with had recently been assigned there. We made it to Fulda late on a snowy afternoon and in our limited German asked directions to the *kaserne*. We were, of course, unaware that there was also a *Bundesgrenzshutz kaserne* in Fulda, but it was to this *kaserne* that we were inadvertently directed. The *Bundesgrenzshutz*, the West German border security force, was the first state armed organization (aside from local police) formed after the war. They had of necessity been outfitted with uniforms left over from the *Wehrmact*. And so it was that we drove around the corner of the road in the late twilight of a snowy afternoon to see a soldier in the uniform and helmet of the World War II *Wehrmact* goose stepping back and forth in front of a red and white striped barrier to the entrance with a red and white striped sentry box at one end. We thought we had been caught in a black and white movie of World War II for a moment. Eventually, we did find our way to the American *kaserne* and then to the off-post quarters of our friends, who were living in an apartment on the economy much like ours. It was a grand reunion and a nice interlude on our drive back to our new home.

Though the army of the 1960s routinely worked until noon on Saturday, even if the unit was in garrison, Saturday night was still a time for relaxing. Some time after we had settled in from our trip north to get our car, and after we could do our own shopping thanks to that car, we invited two couples to our living room of our two-room German apartment for some Saturday night socializing. Though I had been promoted to 1st Lieutenant the previous December, the increase in pay had only brought us to $259.36 a month, so entertaining tended to be very informal with everybody contributing. By coincidence, our landlord and his wife were having a couple in for a little party that same night. Somehow, we all met in the stairwell and were all invited down to their apartment. We brought along our beer and snacks, and they quickly integrated us into their party despite our very limited German and their equally limited English. Fortunately, Jim Hattersley—the executive officer of the tank company to which I had been assigned and one of our invited guests—was fluent in German and helped us bridge the language barrier. As the beer and wine flowed, language became less and less of a problem. It was quite a party! We sang German songs, laughed a lot, and had fun together despite our lack of German fluency. The German people have always been most forgiving of our language skills and have almost always been welcoming. That night was just our first taste of the spontaneous hospitality that was so often extended to the American military serving in Germany in those years.

One of the anomalies of getting to know the German people was that none of the many by then middle age veterans of World War II had ever fought Americans. Invariably, we were told that they had served on the Russian front. The paradox, of course, was that the same folks would tell us with a straight face that they had started learning English when they were prisoners of war in an American prisoner-of-war camp. Though the Russian front had consumed hundreds of German soldiers in a horrific campaign, it seemed apparent that not every veteran we met could have fought there and then learned English when he was our prisoner. It never seemed worthwhile to point out this social inconsistency, which was no doubt intended to avoid a strained conversation with a member of the American military. But we joked about it in private after an evening of socializing with German acquaintances.

After a couple of months, we were able to move on post into temporary quarters on the fourth floor of one of the apartment buildings in which the permanent quarters were located. These apartment buildings had been built to American specifications right after World War II, and the fourth floor apartments had been designed as the maids' quarters in the early days of the occupation. By the time of our arrival, maids were no longer common for junior-officer families because of the vastly improved economy and the elimination of the occupation scrip that had been used as currency. These quarters were now made available as a way station for families waiting for permanent quarters to become available. They had a kitchen, a large living room/dining room area, which had been the common room for the maids, and a string of eight small bedrooms on either side of a long hall. We were able to take delivery of our household goods and set up our home using only a fraction of the space available.

After another few months, we were able to move two flights downstairs to a permanent, furnished, two-bedroom apartment that would be our home for the remainder of our tour. We were in seventh heaven with our accommodations, which had Quartermaster-supplied upholstered furniture in addition to the wooden dining room set we had experienced in our quarters at Fort Knox. Each family had an authorized weight allowance for the shipment of household goods at government expense, which increased according to rank. It was, however, reduced for assignments to Europe as a cost-savings measure. The result was that all of the family-housing apartments in Europe were furnished with Quartermaster-issued furniture that stayed in place as families rotated through the quarters. The issue furniture included stuffed sofas and chairs, a desk, and chests of drawers. Since the styles remained the same, and we got to think that the upholstered coverings did too, we would begin to feel very much at home with this issue furniture before we were through years later.

3

THE POST

Mckee Barracks overlooked the small town of Crailsheim down in the Jagst River valley. A *Luftwaffe* air base had been located there during World War II, and the buildings from that era housed a quartermaster depot of the newly-minted *Bundeswehr* on the far side of the airfield. The depot also trained enlistees and draftees for the *Bundeswehr*, and one or another of the tank companies or artillery batteries stationed on our side of the airfield usually participated in each graduation at the end of their training period. The airfield, which separated the two facilities, was used by our division's light aircraft and helicopters, and was home to a small division aviation section with L19's. These were light fixed-wing aircraft that looked much like a Piper J-3 Cub that were permanently stationed at the field in support of the Combat Command C headquarters, also stationed at McKee Barracks.

The post, or *kaserne*, was located between Highway 14 and the airfield, on the other side of which was the German quartermaster depot. Unlike most of the *kasernes* used by U.S. Forces in Germany, it was not a remnant of the *Wehrmacht*. It had been built during the occupation years by the U.S. Army as the Seventh Army Stockade. As a result, the barracks were two-story stucco structures that replicated the typical wooden barracks of Army posts of that era in the United States. They were laid out in neat blocks, with a central dining facility—called a mess hall in those days—and administrative buildings scattered among the barracks. The only difference from typical barracks buildings was that there were still bars on the windows. The Seventh Army Stockade had been relocated to Mannheim, but the bars had remained when the function of the facility changed. Another remnant of its days as the Seventh Army Stockade was that the family housing area was outside the fence that enclosed the *kaserne*, a feature we would come to appreciate when, some time later, curfews were initiated even for officers.

McKee Barracks was home to Combat Command C of the 4th Armored Division. Combat Commands were a remnant of the World War II armored division and the precursor of the brigade. McKee Barracks also housed the Combat Command's organic tank battalion and its supporting artillery battalion, a self-propelled 105mm howitzer unit. The organic mechanized infantry battalion for the Combat Command was located in Heilbronn, another small town some distance from Crailsheim. Combat Commands were the subordinate units of the division. There were three of them, lettered A through C, each commanded by a colonel. Each had tank battalions, mechanized infantry battalions, and supporting artillery battalions assigned to them. In war, the number and type of battalions assigned to each Combat Command would have depended on the mission and might have changed with each new mission. In peacetime, the structure was permanent.

These combat commands were roughly equivalent to the later brigades or brigade combat teams that have characterized the more recent organization of all army divisions, but it was only the armored divisions that were so organized back then. The infantry divisions of that era had gone "Pentomic," that is, five "Battle Groups," each commanded by a colonel, with five companies each. The armored division organization had been left unchanged from World War II and would be the basis for the brigade organization that would follow, army-wide, in a few years.

The short entrance road from Highway 14 to the *kaserne* split the rectangular enclosure that was McKee Barracks neatly in half. Combat Command headquarters and the Officers Club faced each other just inside the main gate across the entrance road from each other. Prominently located on a concrete pad next to the Officers Club was a World War II Sherman tank named "Cobra King." The 4th Armored Division had been the division to break through into Bastogne to relieve the 101st Airborne Division surrounded there during the Battle of the Bulge. Our tank battalion, the 37th Armor, commanded by then-Lieutenant Colonel Creighton Abrams, had been the lead battalion of the division relief force, and Cobra King had been the lead tank of C Company, the first tank to link up with the surrounded 101st Airborne Division. The meticulously-rehabilitated and maintained replica memorialized one of the battalion's signal successes during World War II.

The half of the post on the Combat Command headquarters side of the entrance belonged to the artillery; the half on the Officers Club side, to the 1-37th Armor, to which I was assigned. Directly in front of the gate, where the entrance road formed a "T" with the first of the parallel interior roads, was a two-story building that housed a small post exchange, a barbershop, a post office, and the noncommissioned officers club. The dispensary (post medical clinic) was located next to this building and a small military police station was located just behind the Combat Command headquarters building. Toward the back of the post were a small commissary for family food shopping, a bowling alley, and the enlisted men's club. Across the road from these buildings and stretching to the back fence that separated the post from the airfield were the motor pools for the tank and artillery battalions. The McKee Barracks portion of the German-American complex was enclosed and separated from the airfield by a high wire fence.

Outside the fence on one end of the rectangle were the family housing area and the Combat Command commander's single-family quarters. Family housing for all but the Combat Command commander consisted of a series of neatly lined up four-story apartment buildings with two stairwells each. Three of the buildings were dedicated to officer families and the rest to noncommissioned officer families. The interior apartments between the stairwells were two-bedroom, and the end apartments were three-bedroom. The fourth floor, previously the maids' quarters, had those gigantic eight-bedroom temporary quarters. So meticulously were these buildings lined up that you could see through eight sets of living rooms and dining rooms if the curtains were not drawn. Each morning, we could see my executive officer, Jim Hattersley, walking around his dining room table on his hands in his apartment in the next row of buildings after we moved into permanent quarters. He had been a gymnast and liked to keep his hand in shape.

The famous meticulousness of the German engineer came into play when we built a baseball diamond at another nearby 4th Armored Division *kaserne* to accommodate the division's baseball competition. The base lines were installed, according to the German engineer interpretation of the plans, as neatly raised curbs before anyone realized what was going on. Needless to say, there was a correction before the first game was played.

4

THE UNIT

The unit to which I was assigned was the 1st Medium Tank Battalion, 37th Armor, known as either the 1-37th Armor or simply the 37th Armor. When I joined, the 37th Armor consisted of three tank companies and a headquarters company. Each tank company had seventeen medium tanks, the M48A1, which mounted a 90mm main gun and was powered by a gasoline engine. The seventeen tanks were divided into three platoons of five tanks each, with two tanks in the headquarters tank section for the company commander and his attached artillery forward observer. At the time, each company also had an infantry squad mounted in an M59 armored personnel carrier for local security and from which to draw replacements in combat for the four-man tank crews. Later during my time with the battalion, a fourth tank company was added in one of the cyclical changes to the basic organization.

There was a small company headquarters section, a maintenance section, and a mess section in the headquarters platoon of each company. Supporting these sections were several 2-1/2 ton trucks and several jeeps, one for the Company Commander when he was not in his tank, one for the First Sergeant, one for the company Executive Officer, and one for the maintenance section. The maintenance section also had a large armored recovery vehicle with winches and booms called a VTR (vehicle, track recovery). These tank companies were compact organizations with little in the way of frills. As a tank platoon leader, I did not have access to a jeep unless I asked to borrow one from the headquarters platoon.

The battalion headquarters company of that era had a tank section for the battalion commander and several staff members and an assortment of wheeled vehicles for the Support Platoon and for the staff officers. There were fuel trucks as well as cargo trucks in the Support Platoon. The battalion's Scout Platoon and Mortar Platoon were also part of the headquarters company, the former manning jeeps mounted with machine guns and the latter manning M59 armored personnel carriers that were factory modified to mount a 4.2-inch mortar on a built-in ring mount (the top deck folded back to enable the mortar to fire from inside the track). The battalion headquarters also had several modified armored personnel carriers with raised roofs that could be parked end to end and connected with tailored lightproof canvas to form the headquarters tactical operations center (TOC) in the field. This type of TOC is still in use in armor, cavalry, and mechanized infantry units, though the vehicles have been updated.

At about the time that the fourth tank company was introduced, the Davy Crockett platoon was added to the battalion headquarters company. The Davy Crockett was a tactical nuclear weapon with a maximum range of about 2.5 miles. The bulbous, unguided, fin-stabilized warhead was fired from a recoilless rifle type launcher in a slow arc, but its nuclear blast would spread instantly lethal radiation for a quarter of a mile from the point of impact and render the area uninhabitable for 48 hours. It was deployed as a defense against the mass infantry and tank attacks that were expected if the Soviets came west, as was the same-size nuclear mine that was deployed at about the same time. We only had high explosive warheads for training, and they were highly inaccurate when fired once a year for qualification. Given the minimum range of the weapon and the projected radius of expected radiation, there was always a question of exactly who would be radiated. Fortunately, the weapon was withdrawn from the inventory without our ever having to find out.

In 1960, the officers in the grade of captain and up that manned the unit were much older than their counterparts would be in my later years. There was a gap of probably twenty years between the ages of the lieutenants and the captains, which was huge when you consider that those lieutenants would make captain in four-and-a-half to five years. Many of the captains of that era had served at the tail end of World War II as junior officers and had been called back for the Korean War, at which point they had decided to stay in until the 20-year retirement point. Though several liked their alcohol a little too well—it was not unusual for a bottle of whiskey to reside in that deep right-hand bottom file drawer common to all government desks—they were a fount of knowledge for junior officers on tanks and on combat. One of these company commanders, as I noted previously, remarked that he never could get used to the German aircraft that gave us mock close air support during training exercises. He always wanted to dive for cover when he saw the iron cross on the underside of their wings.

Some of the captains and the two majors, who were similarly battle tested and slightly older, had been stationed on previous tours in Germany with the occupation forces. They talked about that initial period when dependents were not yet authorized and military scrip was the currency used instead of the deutsche mark. The signing of the official peace treaty in 1955 had ended the occupation era and eliminated scrip, but these folks could tell stories about those early days in the recovery of Germany when a pack of cigarettes would purchase almost anything. They also remembered when the destruction of World War II had been much more obvious, when you could look across the city of Stuttgart and see nothing taller than foundation walls. All that rubble had been collected and piled in one spot to make a huge hill, which was now covered in grass and surmounted by a tower with a revolving restaurant on the top. Few people now remember how that hill in the center of Stuttgart came to be, but even in 1960, you could still see the empty blocks with skeletons of buildings in Nuremberg, Frankfurt, and Würzburg. Though these reminders of the destruction were fast disappearing, they, again, made World War II seem very close to us in those days.

My first battalion commander was an up-through-the ranks lieutenant colonel who was precise, dry, and demanding. He also was a very good tactician and was rarely bested in the annual Army Training Tests. He was followed by an officer who had been commissioned before World War II who was short on field experience and long on staff experience. My third battalion commander was a promotable major on the fast track for promotion by the name of Dale Crittenberger. He was the son of a World War II general, and his older brother would also become a general.

The Crittenbergers had eight children, and Mrs. Crittenberger managed them all in the small confines of an expanded apartment while Major Crittenberger took care of the battalion. There was the traditional welcome for them at the Officers Club when they arrived, with the traditional receiving line so that they could be introduced to the officers and wives of the unit. My wife was very pregnant as we went through the receiving line, and when Major Crittenberger asked her when the baby was due, she quipped, "On D-Day." That drew an uncharacteristic blank from this son of a World War II general, and my wife had to add, "the sixth of June."

We later served with the Crittenbergers on the faculty at West Point. Dale Crittenberger had his promising career cut short when he was killed in a helicopter crash in Vietnam while commanding a brigade in September 1969. His wife died of cancer before all of the children had gained maturity, and his older brother, Major General Willis Crittenberger, resigned before his time in order to fulfill his family obligations. I never knew the general well, though I served on the USAREUR staff when he was the USAREUR Deputy Chief of

Staff for Operations, but I have always thought that his resignation was a fine thing to do for a member of a fine military family.

The 37th Armor occupied roughly half of McKee Barracks, both with regard to the barracks area and the motor pool area. Its central mess hall was located roughly in the middle of the barracks area and its headquarters was located in a two-story building in the center of the post on the edge of the battalion area.

The barracks were filled with a mixture of draftees and regular army enlisted men, with the greater proportion being draftees. Inevitably, the company clerk was the draftee with a college education who kept the first sergeant's records straight. The noncommissioned officers were professionals, many of whom had served in Korea, and the more senior of whom had seen combat in World War II. They might drink a bit too much, but they knew tank gunnery, how to maintain their tanks, and how to position their tanks in the field so that they had good cover and concealment and good fields of fire.

Junior officers, such as myself, rotated through the organization. In the course of a three-year tour, these lieutenants would serve as tank platoon leaders, scout or mortar platoon leaders, company executive officers, and battalion headquarters staff officers. In addition, the lieutenants were assigned a myriad of additional duties on a rotating basis. They served as mess officers, responsible for overseeing the consolidated mess hall in garrison and their own mess sections when in the field, and they served as trial and defense counsels for special courts martial. They paid the troops in cash on the once-a-month paydays and they served as survey officers, responsible for investigating material and equipment losses, and as investigating officers for various alleged offenses. Finally, they served as the Officer of the Day on a rotating basis, manning the battalion headquarters all night, and they served as courtesy patrol officers on weekends, touring the local hot spots to ensure that the soldiers behaved appropriately downtown. It was a busy routine for lieutenants, but it was a wonderful training ground that provided a better background than we realized at the time for our future careers and, eventually, for Vietnam.

The mess officer's responsibility was a training ground that is gone from the Army in this day of contract-dining facilities. In those days, kitchen police (KP) was still an additional duty for soldiers, and the Army served meals from a standardized master menu that was adhered to, and supplies provided for, throughout the Army. In the consolidated mess hall, the company mess sections worked together to produce meals for the entire battalion, served on steel or brown plastic compartmentalized trays.

When we went to the field, the mess sections returned to their parent companies where they typically did their work from a built-up 2-1/2 ton truck that was assigned to the mess section. The canvas and supporting bows were taken off this truck and a plywood structure covered with canvas was mounted on the truck bed. Counters and slots for the three gasoline-fueled field ranges were built in, a side wall was cut out so that it could be propped up to shelter the mess line when serving, and a stair and walkway were manufactured out of wood or pierced steel planking so that the soldiers could be served at truck bed level. The company mess officer supervised all this, but the company cooks took a special pride in besting the other companies in the design and construction of their mess truck and in being able to dress up the field rations to serve a tasty hot meal the moment the unit set up for the night.

C-rations were still very much in use, and some of ours had dates from 1943 and 1945. The odor from a punctured can of eggs with those dates made you want to not eat. And when we went to the field, we ate the C-rations that were part of our basic load on each tank so that we could rotate the stock. On an average day in the field, our cooks would serve a hot breakfast and a hot supper, with C-rations being used for the noon meal. If one of our platoons was located at some distance, we would use insulated mermite cans transported in the first sergeant's jeep and trailer to ensure that our soldiers got to share in the hot meals.

Steel mess kits were still in use for eating in the field, and the mess officer was again responsible for setting up the cleaning line to ensure that good sanitation was maintained. That line consisted of clean, 55-gallon garbage cans filled with water that were heated by gasoline-fueled immersion heaters mounted on the can rims. One way to short circuit a career was for a mess officer to be found during the frequent surprise sanitation inspections to have gotten the wrong order for the pre-rinse, wash, and rinse cans or to not have the water heated to the required temperature. Another risk were the cyclical inspector general or maintenance inspections that always honed in on the crevices and crannies in the gasoline field ranges. Lieutenants learned quickly to pay attention to detail.

Those lessons were carried with us all through the Vietnam days, but by the late 1970s the art of being a Mess Officer had disappeared because of modern individual field rations and contract dining facilities. The result was that when USAREUR headquarters actually went to the field some time in 1979, several of us colonels had to provide instruction on the details of setting up the cleaning line to the captain running the field mess for the headquarters. He had never had to worry about such things in his normal routine.

Lieutenants also acted as trial or defense counsel in special courts martial cases. In those days, the Army lawyers (Judge Advocate General Corps Officers) only worked general courts martial. Lieutenants took turns being assigned as defense counsel and trial counsel (the prosecutor). That worked pretty well, unless the defendant hired a civilian counsel. In one case, I was the trial counsel in the alleged rape of a young woman from Crailsheim. Investigation showed that the young lady was undoubtedly in the business of being paid for her services, but it also showed that on this occasion, she had been forced. With the help of an interpreter, I got the story and some items of clothing whose condition supported her story. I was well prepared to see justice done until the hired civilian defense counsel gave his qualifications at the beginning of the trial, starting with his having been High Commissioner in Berlin most recently and going back over a 3o-year legal career. Needless to say, he made mincemeat out of my case, and the soldier was acquitted.

Nevertheless, we all came out of the courts martial experience knowing the elements of evidence and how to support charges that we might have had to make later in our careers. Lieutenants who had never had that experience always seemed to have trouble understanding the evidence that would be required to support any charges they might need to bring.

Finally, a lieutenant from each company paid the soldiers, who were still paid once a month—in cash, in those days—at a formation called Pay Call. The company lined up in front of the pay officer who sat at a desk with a roster and the cash. When called, the soldier moved to the desk, saluted, gave his name, and was paid in cash according to the roster. The duty of pay officer rotated among the company officers, but when assigned the responsibility, the officer drew ammunition for his .45-caliber pistol and took a jeep to the nearest finance office. There, he was issued the roster and a bag with the money to pay his company. The responsibility of accounting for the money and reconciling the return, if any, after Pay Call belonged entirely to the lieutenant, and a failure in this regard was not a good career move. Oddly, robbery was unheard of and embezzlement was very, very rare. One can only imagine the temptation in today's world. But there was something about the personal connection between the soldier being paid and the leader doing the paying that was good for reinforcing the chain of command. It may be that the far more efficient, and impersonal, centralized pay system and direct deposit of today's Army came at the expense of a personal link between the leader and the led.

Annoying and time consuming as these various additional duties might have been, I am not sure that the Army would not have been better served by preserving what it could of them as "progress" was made in the various responsibilities involved. The opportunity to get a solid grounding in such disparate subjects as military justice and what causes the huge coffee urn in the consolidated mess hall to turn out bitter coffee has been lost over the years.

5

THE TRAINING

The overall mission in those years in USAREUR was to train to go to war on short notice. Our vehicles in the motor pool were combat loaded with their basic load of ammunition and rations. Hard as it is to believe in this day and age, each tank had its main-gun ammunition, its machine gun ammunition, and its crew small-arms ammunition loaded on board in the motor pool. When we went to the annual gunnery qualification courses, we shot up our basic load and replaced it with updated ammunition. The small-arms ammunition we shot up at our local ranges when we did annual qualification firing with small arms. The sturdy issue locks that secured the hatches of each tank were the only security. True, the machine gun and small-arms ammunition were wrapped in canvas and banded with sealed steel strapping—and it was worth a lieutenant's career if the seals were found broken—but there really was nothing to stop the ammunition from vanishing. It simply never happened!

The only incident that ever occurred with a fully combat loaded tank had nothing to do with the ammunition. One night, a tank commander decided he needed to impress a waitress at a local *gasthaus* located at the edge of Crailsheim on a curve in the road that led downhill to the Jagst River. Without setting off an alarm, he somehow managed to drive the tank out the back gate from the motor pool. He drove to the *gasthaus*, intending to do what, we never were sure, but the road was slick with nighttime frost and he could not stop the 48-ton vehicle from sliding toward the *gasthaus*. It stopped with the muzzle of its 90mm main gun sticking through the upper half of the two-piece front door. The sergeant lost a stripe and the door was replaced. The course of true love and all.

Day-to-day training in a tank company consisted of a maintenance period, the morning or the afternoon, and some gunnery instruction: bore sighting, dry fire with fire commands, or subcaliber firing in which the coaxial machine guns mounted parallel to the main gun fired frangible ammunition (the clay-like bullet shattered at impact) at short range targets using the fire control system for the tank's main gun. There was also physical training and classroom instruction on chemical, biological and nuclear warfare, first aid, map reading, and similar soldier skills. But the major training took place in the field.

The "Alert" was the major training vehicle when we were in garrison. At least twice a month, Alerts were called. They could be "stand-by" Alerts, where the unit mustered in full field gear, weapons drawn from the arms room, and merely reported to their vehicles ready to move out. It was always a timed event—two hours to be ready to move out. After each unit had reported that it was ready to move and had established communications on the various radio nets, there might or might not be some sort of inspection (fuel and oil levels in the tanks, condition of the basic load, or some other area of interest of the moment) and then we would stand down, turn in weapons, and pick up the training schedule for that day.

The more frequent Alerts were "move-out" Alerts. Close to every *kaserne* in Germany was a dispersal area that provided cover for the unit away from its permanent station that would be a preplanned target for the Soviets in the event of war. These dispersal areas were anywhere from a couple of miles to ten miles from the post, depending on the terrain. There was a maximum time allowed for the unit to move to the dispersal area (depending on the distance involved), set up a perimeter, and establish radio contact. In event of war, it would be from these dispersal areas that the units would move forward to their general alert defensive positions much closer to the interzonal border between East and West Germany.

Simultaneously with the unit alert announcement, the military police would tour the family housing areas announcing that it was a practice alert, but that had it been the real thing, the Noncombatant Evacuation Order for dependents would have been implemented. That order directed that each private vehicle must be kept at least half full of gasoline and that each family must have rations for three days available to take with them (most people usually purchased a case of C-rations from the commissary and left it in the hall coat closet against that eventuality). Each family had a map and each family was supposed to have driven the "noncombatant evacuation route" so that they were familiar with it. This aspect was rather less inspected than the unit move-out.

In later years, a sticker on the private vehicle windshield took the place of the loudspeaker announcement for the military families, but there was always the loudspeaker jeep to announce the alert to the military members of the family. Simultaneously, phone alerts initiated by the duty officer at battalion headquarters would go out to key personnel and to personnel living off post. Each key person had a list of names to notify and there was a notification tree for those living off post, even if they did not have a phone in their German apartment.

These move-out Alert training exercises were high-pressure events for all concerned. Meeting the time schedules was all important, and more than a few careers were short stopped because the unit could not get organized, draw weapons, and arrive at the dispersal area by the appointed time. USAREUR initiated the majority of the alerts, but Seventh Army, the Division Headquarters, or the Combat Command Headquarters could also initiate them for units in their respective commands. The result was that you could never be sure that you were finished for the month after one or two Alerts. They almost always came at 4 a.m. The phone would ring, and you were off in the pre-dawn darkness, regardless of what the training schedule said had been planned for the day. Recovering from a move-out Alert would take the rest of the day after the Alert was terminated. And then, there was always the possibility that it was not a practice, which led to another level of tension.

With the central part that these Alerts played in our lives, it was inevitable that they became the stuff of stories. One story had to do with the tank battalion that was stationed at a *kaserne* in the middle of Munich shortly after the Occupation officially came to an end. The first time a 4 a.m. move-out Alert was called, the tank battalion moved out to its dispersal area and found that it had a great deal of company on the roads. It was close enough in time to World War II, and there were sufficient East-West tensions, that the good residents of Munich were taking no chances when they heard the familiar noise of tanks moving. They decided to move too. That tank battalion never moved out on an Alert again and was soon relocated to a more rural area.

And then there was my classmate from the Armor Officer Basic Course who had been assigned to a border armored cavalry regiment. The border regiments overwatched the border with a combination of observation posts and motorized patrols. A platoon would be sent to an observation post for a tour of patrol duty, and the platoon leader would set up the platoon headquarters there. His machine gun-jeep-mounted scout section would then make motor patrols along prescribed, but varied, routes that enabled the platoon to cover the entire border in its assigned sector in a random way. If a border crossing by tanks in more than platoon strength was observed, the platoon leader was required to report it immediately, and that report would trigger a USAREUR-wide move-out Alert.

My former classmate had his platoon on the border one day and was watching the border from his observation post when he saw a column of tanks approaching the border from the east. The tanks were moving down a dirt track directly toward the border, which was then demarked only by border stones in those days, with a 10-meter wide plowed strip of dirt reaching back from it on the east side. Closer and closer they came. Finally, the lead tank closed to within a few yards of the plowed strip. The lieutenant picked up the phone and made the report. He then looked up to see the column make a right turn and drive off on a nearly invisible dirt track, parallel to the plowed strip and the border on the back east edge of the plowed strip. Too late! All USAREUR units were in the process of starting to assemble for the move to their dispersal areas. Again, such initiative was not particularly good for one's career, although if he had been wrong and they were attacking, it might have been even worse for all involved.

Another never-to-be-repeated Alert resulted when the powers that be thought that it would be a good thing to test the units on New Year's Eve. That one was talked about for years afterwards, but was never repeated. My wife and I were at the Officers Club with the rest of the post complement for the traditional celebration when, close to midnight, the Alert was called. The officers quickly escorted their wives the short distance to quarters and then prepared to move their units out. By that time, I was commanding A Company. I had remained fairly sober, but not so the rest of my company. We made it to our tanks in some fashion and got the radio net established, but the move to the dispersal area was not a very orderly road march. There were tanks all over the road and off the edges of the road, and the chaos was supervised by officers whose blue, gold-striped dress uniform trousers stuck out below their olive drab winter parkas. It was not a pretty sight. Fortunately, at least in our battalion, there were no injuries, and only some bent fenders on the tanks, which was a miracle. Thereafter, Alerts were never called on New Year's Eve.

Of course, I had to make my own contribution to Alert lore. Shortly after I had been given my company command as a 1st Lieutenant, we had a routine move-out Alert. The tanks and tracked vehicles moved by one route to the dispersal area, and the wheeled vehicles used another, less rugged route. After supervising my tank platoons move through the back gate and out toward the dispersal area under their respective leaders, I gathered up the supply truck, mess truck, and water trailer, which had been loaded out while the tanks were getting ready to move, and led them out the front gate and down Highway 14 to a side road that led to our dispersal area. A short distance from the wooded area where my tanks were taking up their positions, the access road crossed a set of railroad tracks. This early morning, the red and white barrier was down, blocking our way. We raised the barrier into a vertical position by hand and drove over the tracks, but the built-up mess truck was too high, and the corner of its roof caught the not-quite-vertical elevated barrier and broke it. We calmly laid it down by the side of the road and went about our business.

The rest of the Alert went well and we were back in the motor pool by about noon. My supervision of our after-operation maintenance and refueling was interrupted by a summons from the Combat Command Commander to report to his office. It seemed that a broken railroad barrier sent a signal to the railroad yards that prevented trains from moving until the problem was fixed. Our small accident had immobilized the vaunted *Bundesbahn* train system in southern Germany for most of the morning and there were a number of people who were not pleased with my initiative to get my mess truck to the company dispersal area—my Combat Command Commander, a very austere full colonel, amongst them.

6

THE MAJOR TRAINING AREAS

The major training areas in West Germany figured almost as largely in our lives as the Alert process. Grafenwoehr Training Area, located in northern Bavaria to the northwest of Nuremberg, was a sprawling maneuver and firing range complex. At the southern end of the reservation was Vilseck which was the Combined Arms Training Center for Seventh Army where various technical, maintenance, and leadership courses were conducted. Further south, and southwest of Nuremberg, was the Hohenfels Training Area, a hilly 40,000-acre maneuver area with more than fifty ranges for collective unit training. Its primary use was as an armor and infantry maneuver area. There was also a smaller collective training area at Wildflecken, located midway between Fulda on the north and Bad Kissingen on the south, which supported live fire training for armor, mechanized infantry, and artillery units; and still another training area at Baumholder, which was used primarily by the 8th Infantry Division. Wildflecken was not much used by our division's units, so it was not until years later that I had any experience with it.

In the 1960s, tank units spent two firing periods at Grafenwoehr annually and one maneuver period at either Grafenwoehr or Hohenfels. These major training areas were also the settings for the annual tank crew qualification firing at Grafenwoehr and the annual unit training tests at either Grafenwoehr or Hohenfels.

Failure at either was career threatening for a commander at any level. The typical stay at a major training area for either maneuver or firing was four to five weeks. The result of that was something like 120 days in the field away from home garrison annually, though that number usually included a major war game in which one or another division from one corps opposed another division from the other corps, complete with opposing armored cavalry regiments.

The units moved their tracked vehicles to Grafenwoehr or Hohenfels by train, while the wheeled vehicles moved by road convoy. Rail loading was another career threatening opportunity. The unit would move to the local railhead and load the tanks on flatbed rail cars. The tank tracks could overhang the edges of the flatbed rail cars by only a prescribed amount, checked carefully by the ever-vigilant *Bundesbahn* railroad professionals. Once the placement of the tanks on these rail cars was approved, the vehicles were tied down with cables. Any tank that could not move in the midst of this organized chaos would hold up the unit and interfere with the *Bundesbahn* train schedules. Once the vehicles were loaded, the soldiers boarded the attached passenger cars for the trip. Upon arrival at the major training area rail siding, the process was repeated in reverse, with fingers crossed that each tank would start so that it could be driven off the flatbed rail cars without any delay.

My first trip to Grafenwoehr in late winter of 1960 was a bit of a shock. The word "primitive" comes to mind, though we all survived nicely. I was then a tank platoon leader in A Company, and my tanks got loaded and off-loaded without incident. We then road marched from the railhead to our temporary track park, which was a sea of mud. The battalion, soldiers and company-grade officers alike, were quartered in concrete single-story barracks built in the 1950s and heated by an iron potbellied stove. There was no running water. These barracks were clustered in battalion-size "field camps" located adjacent to the motor pools and track parks, which had easy access to the main tank trail. The only concession to the company-grade officers was that they were all accommodated together in one of the concrete barracks buildings. The interiors were alike for all buildings: canvas army cots lined up facing each other along the walls, no partitions, and the iron potbellied stove at one end of the barracks. The common sinks and showers were in one centrally located concrete wash house, and the common toilets, lined up facing each other along the walls without any partitions or doors, were in another separate concrete latrine building. The trick, of course, was to get to either facility without sinking ankle-deep in the mud. Shower clogs were not the thing and were easily lost in the goo.

There was also a central mess hall for the battalion and a smaller building for the battalion headquarters. Company orderly rooms were set up at one end of a troop barracks that was usually dedicated to the company senior noncommissioned officers, with a temporary partition made out of raw white muslin "target cloth" to separate the office from the senior-noncommissioned-officer living space. It was pretty primitive. And the irony is that these same training areas—completely modernized, refurbished, and rebuilt with newly constructed family housing units added—are the locus for the current large-hub installations that house the troops that remain in Germany. What a change fifty years makes!

Grafenwoehr had been a German army training facility since 1907, having been established by the sovereign monarchy of Bavaria during the German Confederation period. It covered approximately 90-square miles and had been used for refugee and prisoner-of-war camps immediately after World War II from 1945 to 1947, when the U.S. Army reactivated it for collective unit training. The permanent-party troop accommodations had been built in the early 1900s, slightly updated with modern plumbing over the years. The main post complex also dated from that era and was comprised of a mixture of two-story stucco and wood buildings in the original

Franconian style and the later concrete two-story buildings. Some of these buildings had been turned into administrative offices and classrooms, as well as the permanent-party barracks. Some were also reserved as bachelor officer quarters for the field grade officers of the visiting battalions.

The Training Center commander's quarters and the landmark water tower that loomed over it in the center of the main post dated from 1908 and were both in the quaint Bavarian style. The house had the typical gingerbread wood fretwork, shutters, and a railed porch running around the house. In my first year of training visits to Grafenwoehr, Colonel Burba, the commander, was an old horse cavalryman. He toured the close-in tank ranges and training areas on horseback, and if you passed his quarters at noon, you would see his horse tethered to the porch railing. The 135-foot turreted water tower that loomed over it had become the antenna platform for the Armed Forces Network radio, and later the TV station, and the guidance beacon for the Grafenwoehr Army Airfield.

The interior of the 90-square mile training reservation was a rolling, hilly area that had been pretty well denuded of any foliage. It was enclosed by a well-graded dirt tank trail that was pounded by tracked vehicles day and night. The result was that it was either muddy or dusty, and the transition would start as soon as the rain stopped or started. What little vegetation that remained existed in the margin between the perimeter tank trail and the outer training reservation boundary. It was much in demand for overnight *lagers* (temporary encampments) during our maneuver training, though it was also home to herds of wild boar that could rampage through the mess area. These boars were also known to attack the unwary person on foot on occasion.

There was also a tank trail that bisected the reservation. Spotted along the perimeter tank trail just south of the main post were the stationary tank ranges where bore sighting and zeroing took place, as well as the initial stationary qualification ranges of the annual tank qualification course. That course was divided into eight "tables," and Tables I through V, the stationary tables, were fired on these ranges. Table VI, a moving machine gun table, was fired further out on the perimeter tank trail, and Tables VII and VIII were fired from ranges off of the bisecting tank trail where the tanks could fire their main guns into a safe impact area in the center of the reservation.

Tables VII and VIII were moving tables where each tank drove over a prescribed course and engaged a variety of targets with both the main gun and machine guns. They were fired both day and night, using the tank-mounted searchlights and illumination rounds at night. Table VIII on Range 42 was the dreaded tank crew proficiency course that marked the tank, the platoon, the company, and the battalion as a success or a failure based on a passing score and the number of tanks in the respective units that passed. So highly competitive was the process that even passing was a marginal accomplishment if the score, or aggregate scores, were not sufficiently high. Tank gunnery was a serious matter and the culmination of the year's worth of training that led up to it.

My first visit to Grafenwoehr was for maneuver training, so we were scheduled into various maneuver areas for several days at a time. We would practice the various phases of attack and defense: the approach march with an emphasis on hitting designated check points and the line of departure on time to the minute, the attack of some hill that served as an objective (typically surmounted by the remains of an observation tower or an old bunker), defense of the hill after we occupied it, and eventually a delaying action back to a *lager* area. The destroyed bunkers dated from World War II when the famous Siegfried Line was being constructed. One bunker of each type had been built at Grafenwoehr for strength testing purposes. The bunkers had passed the test by absorbing the demolition attempts and the brooding remnants served as our landmarks.

After several days of this, we would return to the field camp area to clean up ourselves and our equipment, do the maintenance required to augment the basic maintenance that went on continuously in the field, critique the tactics and positioning of the tanks that had taken place, and then go out and do it again. The delay and passing through friendly lines, usually at night, was one of the techniques that we practiced the most because it was assumed that if the Russians ever attacked, we would have to defend and delay until we could concentrate sufficient reinforcements from the United States to counterattack. The result of this repetitive training was that the proper positioning of a tank for maximum cover and concealment in any terrain and precision timing in road marching became second nature.

Later, in 1961, after General James K. Polk took command of the division, I was to take part in the ultimate demonstration of precision timed road marching. By then I was commanding A Company and could better understand what we had learned in all those days in the field. General Polk's roots were in cavalry, and much later I was to learn that the horse cavalry regiments of the 1930s had a culmination to their training year that he brought to the 4th Armored Division in the 1960s. In the late 1930s, the graduation exercise for the year's training had the four regiments of the "square" 1st Cavalry Division of that era starting from different locations on a road march that would cross the regiments at an intersection and then mass them at a parade location where the entire division of four regiments would conduct a mounted pass-by.

General Polk brought that to the 4th Armored Division when twice during my tour with the division, all 3,000 vehicles and all 14,000 troopers conducted a mounted pass-by in one of the open, relatively flat areas at Grafenwoehr. As with the horse cavalry, the routes of march of the battalions were timed to cross at intersections, with one battalion crossing its tanks between the other in the 100-

yard standard march interval between tanks. We all then gathered at the pass-by area and formed five tanks abreast by battalion to pass in review. It was an awe-inspiring, dusty sight, and the Lord help the commander whose tank fell out because of maintenance problems during the pass in review. We later practiced this crossing exercise in some of the major opposing forces exercises that were conducted off the reservation.

One of the interesting aspects of road marching tanks at Grafenwoehr was the range of the M48A1 tank. It got fourteen gallons to the mile — yes, *gallons* to the mile. To augment the integral gas tanks, four 55-gallon drums were mounted on brackets on the rear of the tank. With that capacity, a tank could get around the perimeter of the reservation just about once, depending on the tank. Refueling and judging when to refuel were very big issues because the ironclad lore of the Armor Corps was that the ultimate embarrassment for any tank commander or officer was to run out of fuel. The challenge was made even greater by the fact that some tanks would average the fourteen gallons to the mile and some would not get even that. The trick was to know which tank did what and to plan accordingly for refueling.

There was, of course, an officers' club at the main post, and when we came back to our base camps from our training in the maneuver areas, it was the place to gather. When I first arrived, it was a pretty cramped facility, mostly a bar with a small dining area done in dark wood. Later in that first tour, a large, modern dining room was added, but the original dining area remained part of the bar for socializing and for a light meal. It was a loud and friendly place in which to relax and have a beer and a hamburger after living out in the dust and mud.

You could not go there without finding an officer with whom you had gone to school with, either pre-commission or the Armor Officer Basic Course, which all new lieutenants attended as their initial assignment in the Army. It was a place to catch up on family news and to tell stories of tank training. It was also a place to bring your wife on the rare occasions that some slack in our training schedule over a weekend offered some free time and allowed her to come up for a couple of days. There were no accommodations for junior officers and their visiting spouses on the post at Grafenwoehr, so we spread out to the little towns and the *gasthauses* that offered a room, probably over the chicken yard, and a shared bathroom down the hall. On one occasion, shortly after the new dining room had opened, my wife and I were seated along a wall when a mouse ran by our table. My wife remarked on it to our German waiter, who replied, without missing a beat, that it was a *haustier*—a house pet.

On another occasion, my wife and another wife had driven up and were going to stay an additional night in our *gasthaus* after my brief pass ended on Sunday evening so that they could drive back to Crailsheim in daylight. Unfortunately, we had filled up our 1954 Ford with quartermaster gasoline on post. In those days, you could buy quartermaster gasoline on post for ten cents a gallon or purchase coupons that allowed you to buy Esso gasoline on the economy for a bit more, twenty-one cents for regular and twenty-three cents for high test. The quartermaster gasoline frequently had water in it, and it had gotten quite cold on the night in question. The next morning, I had a frantic phone call telling me that the gas lines had frozen up. I and the other husband were allowed off post to take care of the problem before resuming our training schedule, but we never again used quartermaster gasoline in our own vehicles after that. And, yes, even officers needed a pass to leave the training area when the unit was training in those days.

A year or so later, when I was a company commander, one of my new platoon leaders had trouble finding a place to stay for himself and his very pregnant wife. For some reason, that particular weekend had brought a number of wives to visit, and the local *gasthauses* were filled up, causing him to go further afield than usual. He ended up going all the way to Weiden in der Oberpfalz, a border town with a large U.S. Army presence because it was the location of a border camp for the 2nd Armored Cavalry Regiment. There he located a hotel that had a room. During the registration, the clerk asked him if the room was "*mit frau*." My lieutenant said yes, thinking that the clerk was just confirming that the room was for he and his wife. Apparently his tentative German fluency had caused a misunderstanding because shortly after the lieutenant and his wife got settled into the room, there was a knock on the door. When he opened the door, he found the *frau* that he had ostensibly asked for—a fine looking local hooker who was well used to providing company for soldiers. The incident was food for joking for some time, and the lieutenant was more cautious in his answers to questions asked in German thereafter.

When we returned to McKee Barracks at Crailsheim, I had a new assignment. The battalion Scout Platoon leader position had become vacant, and thanks to my experience in the 6th Armored Cavalry Regiment, I was assigned to the position. I would come back to A Company some eight months later, but I moved to the Headquarters Company, to which the Scout Platoon belonged, to become the eyes and ears of the battalion.

7

THE SCOUT PLATOON

The Scout Platoon of that era was mounted in fourteen jeeps. There were three scout sections of four jeeps each, each mounting a .3o-caliber machine gun on a pedestal mount that was centered on the floor just behind the two front seats. Each jeep was manned by a driver, a vehicle commander, and a machine gunner. There was also a jeep and trailer for the platoon sergeant and a jeep for the platoon leader. While these vehicles would not give great protection from enemy fire, or the improvised explosive device (IEDs) that have become so prevalent in Iraq and Afghanistan, they were simple enough that the troopers could devote most of their time to scouting skills. As scout vehicles became more heavily armored to protect the occupants and more complex as technology evolved, more time has been devoted to maintenance and gunnery and less to scouting skills.

These scouting skills were focused primarily on road reconnaissance techniques and the creation of obstacles since the Scout Platoon would lead the way for the tank battalion in the advance and trail the battalion in a retrograde operation such as the delay. The scouts had to be expert in assessing roads and bridges for their tank-carrying capability, in finding terrain that would support tank traffic if the roads or bridges were inadequate, and in ensuring that there was sufficient clearance between the buildings of the small towns we went through to allow passage of our tanks. In short, a clear route forward for the battalion was the Scout Platoon's responsibility. There was always the hovering fear that our platoon would lead the battalion onto a bridge that would collapse, thus stalling the whole column, or into a town whose streets were so narrow that they would not allow passage of the lead tank, leaving the entire battalion in the position of having to somehow turn around or back out. For a Scout Platoon leader, there was the sure knowledge that he would make that mistake only once.

In a retrograde operation, the platoon had to be expert in knowing how to blow key bridges and establish hasty tank obstacles to delay an advancing enemy. The focus was on giving the tank companies the maximum time to prepare their next delay position, but its overall role was to assist the battalion in trading maximum time for minimum terrain so that the enemy would be delayed in its advance to the maximum—and provide the time needed for reinforcements to arrive in Europe before the Soviet Bloc forces could make sufficient headway to make those reinforcements irrelevant.

Finally, the platoon had to be expert in using terrain to maneuver so as not to unnecessarily expose its unarmored vehicles in order to survive on the battlefield. Terrain appreciation and map reading were a huge part of scouting, and nobody who ever served as a scout ever found himself at a loss with maps in later years. Map reading and the use of a compass were stressed because the potential impact of failure in these areas, even in training, was much more real than some of the theoretical training impacts of misreading the influence of wind on radiological fallout. One had only to witness fifty-one tanks making a U-turn and reversing direction to understand the embarrassment of having led a tank battalion down the wrong road or having made the wrong turn at an intersection. Such a mistake usually happened only once to a Scout Platoon leader, and the pressure to be right all the time was strong. Such was life before GPS.

I also found myself being sent to a variety of schools that supported other required scouting skills of the era, such as a Chemical, Biological, and Radiological (CBR) Instructor Course or an Explosive Ordnance Reconnaissance Course. The former was to provide expertise for our responsibility as the battalion's monitor of the use of chemical or biological agents against the battalion and as the battalion's monitor of potential radiological fallout from either enemy or friendly nuclear weapons should it come to that. The latter was to learn how to find and disarm mines and booby traps that scouts might encounter in leading the battalion forward. While our gunnery responsibilities were a fraction of what the tank platoons had to worry about, the sheer breadth of the skill sets that we were supposed to be expert in kept us just as busy.

In that summer and fall of 1960, President Eisenhower was intent on reducing the size and the budget of the U.S. Army, and fuel was at a premium. To this day, I have a vivid memory of walking down the airfield with the entire platoon pretending that we were in our vehicles. There we were with the driver, vehicle commander, and gunner walking in the positions they would be sitting in if they were in their scout jeeps while we practiced moving our pretend vehicles into various tactical formations. Not very thrilling!

Alerts were still high-pressure events for us because we had to get out ahead of the battalion to act as road guides, which meant we had to load up and move out even more quickly than the tank companies. While loading up a jeep was not a major problem, rigging for the field took some time. It was an article of faith that you could not go into combat with any canvas—the top, the side curtains, or the door—still up on the jeep. In addition, the windshield had to be lowered and covered with canvas so that it would not reflect light. Those lessons stuck with me when I was a company commander, a squadron executive officer in Vietnam, and a squadron commander in West Germany later. No wheeled vehicles in my command ever went to the field or into combat with canvas up, which made for some very cold and wet work. It also meant, however, that you were always in tune with your surroundings.

Two other practices followed me through my career after my stint as the Scout Platoon leader: I never could tolerate any vehicle, armored or not, poking its nose over a hill or around a corner without stopping in a position that was still concealed to find out what lay ahead. The jeeps were just too vulnerable to even machine gun fire to take that chance, and the precaution paid dividends in my units in later years. The second practice was to always install a pedestal mount in my jeep whether or not I had a machine gun to go with it. It acted like a roll bar if you rolled over, and it saved my life a year later when we were issued new, lighter jeeps that had a greater tendency to roll.

While battalion maneuver periods at Grafenwoehr were exciting times for the Scout Platoon, the tank gunnery periods were not. Since we had no tank guns, we were liable for road guard and range guard duty, which was cold and boring, though a necessary safety precaution to prevent the unwary from wandering into live fire impact areas by mistake. These range details were levied on all of the training units, so it was a fact of life. Fortunately, my first visit to Grafenwoehr with the Scout Platoon was for the battalion's annual Army Training Test (ATT). This was a rigorous culmination to the year's training that was conducted over four days and four nights and covered the typical tactical situations that would be required of the battalion in combat. We spent the first weeks of our stay at Grafenwoehr maneuvering back and forth over the churned terrain in practice for the actual test.

The Scout Platoon acted as a screen in the advance after leading the battalion to the line of departure using road reconnaissance techniques, screened the battalion from the enemy on a flank during the attack, kept contact with flank units (represented by umpires) during the defense, and set obstacles and blew bridges in front of the battalion during the delay back prior to passing through friendly lines (represented by umpires, again). After several weeks of this intense practice, with a critique after each operation, we ran the actual test against the mechanized infantry battalion from our Combat Command, which was also undergoing its ATT. The organization for the test had our battalion attaching a tank company to the opposing mechanized infantry battalion and it attaching an infantry company to our battalion. This "cross-reinforcing" was routine and reflected the doctrine that tanks usually would operate with supporting infantry and visa versa.

During this period, my battalion commander was a lieutenant colonel who had come through World War II and Korea and would disappear from the Army after this command as far as I knew. He may well have been promoted to colonel, but I never encountered him nor heard his name again. Promotion or not, he was close to the end of his career. The opposing mechanized infantry battalion was commanded by a West Point lieutenant colonel, who had been the first in his class to be promoted to lieutenant colonel and was destined to become a lieutenant general. He was ably assisted by another West Pointer, a major who served in the dual capacity of his operations officer and his executive officer, and who would be a major general. Both had taught in the elite social science department during my cadet days. The lesson that I learned from this apparently unequal match was most interesting.

Time after time, this opposing force led by these two very smart and competent professionals would initiate a complex maneuver that was both creative and tactically sound. And time after time, my battalion commander would manage a simple response that got us to commanding terrain in time to thwart the opposing battalion's tactics. Whatever his background and promotion potential, my battalion commander had mastered basic tank warfare in the hard school of experience. I never forgot that lesson.

8

THE COMPANY

In January 1961, the recently arrived A Company commanding captain developed a medical condition that prevented him from spending extended time in the field exposed to cold weather. As a result, a vacancy came open and I was selected to command A Company as a 1st lieutenant. It was a wonderful opportunity and a huge challenge, but I looked forward to it. I felt very fortunate to have been given the opportunity to command a company as a 1st lieutenant. I had watched as 1st lieutenants, who were considerably senior to me, rotated back to the U.S. after a three-year tour without ever having had the opportunity to command a company because there was a surfeit of captains to fill any company command slots that came open. Jim Hattersley, who was commissioned two years ahead of me in 1956 and had been the A Company executive officer when I commanded my tank platoon, had won the coveted Draper Leadership Award with that same platoon before I arrived, had never had the opportunity to be more than the second in command. I had hoped for such an opportunity, but I had not been optimistic.

For the next fifteen months, I would have the privilege of commanding just over 100 men, seventeen tanks, the miscellaneous organic tracked and wheeled vehicles that we used to support our tanks, and one German Shepherd mascot named "Jeep W. Tank." (Unfortunately, I had to relieve our mascot of his duties after he bit the battalion commander during a visit of that august personage to our company area.) During my tour of command, we would conduct several tank gunnery qualification cycles and several Army Training Test cycles. A Company would place second in the division in both the tank gunnery qualification and the Armor Leadership Award competition, which was based on the high score in the Army Training Test. We would also participate in several major maneuvers in which one division faced another division in mock combat over the back roads and through the forests and small towns of Germany. These carried names such as "Autumn Shield" (for the time of year that it was conducted) and "Peacemaker" (after the Berlin Wall went up).

Our tanks were M48A1's. The "48" represented the year that they were accepted into the Army inventory. By the time that I arrived, they had been through twelve years of hard service. Each tank mounted a 90mm main gun, a .30-caliber coaxial machinegun, and an externally mounted .50-caliber machine gun in front of the tank commander's hatch. That M2 Browning .50 caliber is still with us today, and it was not new in 1960. These tanks were powered by gasoline engines. The technology of the period and the age of the vehicles allowed a lot of gas to escape during start-up, and gasoline flare-ups were not unusual. The wrong thing to do was to cut the engine and allow the flames to take hold. Better to gun the engine so that the cooling fan would blow out the flames. And then there was the "little Joe," a pull-start auxiliary engine used to keep the batteries charged so that the radios could be on continuously when the main engine was turned off and to supply a spark if the batteries were low. It, too, could be the source of a gasoline flare-up in some circumstances.

The sights and range finder were the same as had been on the M41 light tank from my 6th Armored Cavalry days, and the "flying geese" optical sights still required the tank commander to be able to see in "stereo" in order to range properly. There was, however, an enhancement on the M48 that enabled the gunner to simply index the super elevation (the extra elevation peculiar to the type of ammunition to be fired that had to be added to the main gun elevation required for the determined range) for the different types of ammunition through mechanical cams controlled by a "T" handle located next to the gunner's seat. This crude "computer" consisted of a series of cams for the different types of ammunition available. The cams, in a box bolted to the turret wall from which the "T" handle extended, were linked mechanically to the main gun elevation system and changed the angle of the gun beyond what the raw range to the target required.

The first tank gunnery qualification cycle that I experienced as a company commander was also the last Seventh Army Gunnery Program to be conducted. This "Bergen-Hohne Shoot" had been held for the past six years at the British tank gunnery ranges, known by the acronym NORTHAG (Northern Army Group) Ranges, located next to Bergen in the British zone in northern Germany. It was a highly competitive shoot, hosted by a different USAREUR division each year, and it was about to become history because of the move toward decentralization in training. Decentralization, emphasizing responsibility and authority for the small unit leader, meant that future gunnery qualification cycles would be conducted by each division during its own annual training at the major training areas.

Bergen is located north of Hanover on what is called the Lüneburg Heath, a rather bleak area of sparse spruce trees and stunted birch trees. It is prone to misty rain and fog that frequently caused tank firing to be suspended because of low visibility. The railhead for the ranges at Bergen-Hohne was located in the center of Bergen, so we off-loaded our tanks there in the center of town and road marched out to the range complex. Four miles to the southwest of Bergen was Bergen-Belsen, one of Hitler's infamous concentration camps. One day when firing had been suspended because of a steady drizzle and low-hanging clouds, my driver and I took my jeep and drove to Bergen-Belsen.

We drove back to the center of Bergen and then out on another road to the site of the camp.

Still visible as we drove through the camp were a number of grass-covered dirt humps that were the mass graves and the machine gun alleys where the prisoners had been lined up to be executed. There was also a lovely modernistic monument that explained in thirteen languages what had taken place here. The surroundings were, aside from the monument, largely as they had been. Though most of the buildings had been leveled, their foundation outlines were clearly visible, and the camp setup was easily identifiable. There were even a couple of broken-down buildings still standing. The site, of course, was totally deserted on this wet, foggy spring day. It took very little imagination to visualize what had taken place at this bleak camp in chilly, damp north Germany, and it took no imagination at all to know that the good citizens of Bergen could not have been ignorant of what went on here. The prisoners were off-loaded at the same centrally located railhead that we had used to off-load our tanks, and the prisoners would then have been marched out from the center of town to the camp four miles away. Knowledge of the atrocities that took place was obviously not a question if you lived in Bergen; what might have been done with that knowledge is another question that I leave to others. More than fifty years later, the memory of the details of my first company gunnery competition have pretty well faded. The memory of the Nazi concentration camp and its juxtaposition with Bergen has not.

"Autumn Shield" was the first of the major maneuvers that I participated in and the last one in which we used our M48A1 tanks, which would be exchanged for the new M60s shortly after the exercise. These exercises typically started near the major training areas where an entire division could be assembled. We would arrive at the training area, go through some rigorous training in preparation for the exercise and then kick it off. The area between Grafenwoehr and Hohenfels was a frequent mock battleground, with the training areas offering the opportunity for free, off-road maneuver for the tracked vehicles, which were otherwise constrained to roads and specified wooded areas for our overnight *lagers* out of consideration for the potential maneuver damage to the farmland in what was still rural West Germany.

Despite the attention paid to maneuver damage, I have often thought that our German hosts were far more tolerant than the folks living outside Fort Hood, Texas, would ever have been. One night during "Autumn Shield," we had been engaged in a delaying action after a hypothetical violation of the West German border. That meant that we gave ground grudgingly and made local counterattacks to set the opposing force back on its heels. We were making a night road march to a line of departure for one of those counterattacks when we came up to a typical German farm village, a cluster of stone buildings arrayed along narrow streets with no sidewalks. I drove into the town in my jeep in order to make sure we could get through. It looked pretty tight to this ex-Scout Platoon leader. I radioed my finding to battalion headquarters and returned to the head of my company column to find my battalion commander—not the experienced tanker of our Army Training Test—waiting for me. He assured me that we could move forward and that division would not have routed us this way if the town were impassable to tanks. We had a short discussion of what I had seen, and then I was peremptorily ordered to move out.

By then it was getting on to 2 a.m., and the noise of the tank column echoing in the narrow streets should have ensured that no villager was still asleep. The column of tanks moved slowly forward until it came to the center of town where the buildings around the central square were set at an angle to the street we were on. The lead tank slowly headed into the gap and I watched in horror as the end connectors on the tracks caught on the leading edges of the buildings on either side and started to climb the walls of both buildings. The physics of the situation was against the old stone buildings holding out against the weight of a 5o-ton tank for long, and both walls started to crumble in, opening the interior living spaces to the night. We stopped our forward progress rather quickly and backed out—fortunately, the buildings did not cave in, though there was a lot of fresh air rushing into them—and found another way to our objective. I am sure that the townspeople were reimbursed handsomely for the damage we did, but I couldn't escape the feeling that the good residents of Killeen, Texas, outside of Fort Hood, might not have been so accommodating about their broken sleep and broken houses. I suspect we might have needed our armor protection against the shotgun pellets!

If that seems farfetched, I have a vivid memory of my flight school days at Camp Gary, Texas, which was located outside of San Marcos, just southeast of Austin. The Army's fixed wing flight school was located there, and the air was filled with single-engine, two-seater L19 light planes in the hands of student pilots with the instructor sitting behind them. South of the camp was a large chicken farm located under one of the patterns for the training flights. The chicken farmer believed that the noise of the planes upset the laying habits of his hens, and he demonstrated his unhappiness with that situation by firing a shotgun at any plane that happened to fly over the farm. More than a few L19's came back to land with shotgun pellets marking the underside of their wings. It was cosmetic damage to be sure, but it was nevertheless a bit unsettling to the student pilots. If that kind of reaction could be evoked by the supposed interference with the hens laying their eggs, one can only imagine what the reaction would be to a half-destroyed home.

"Autumn Shield" did, however, provide me with a dramatic demonstration of what a well-trained unit can look like when it goes into action, which was the goal of all this training, after all. We put a lot of store in hand and arm signals in those days instead of relying so much on radios, so it was not unusual for us to move out without so much as a radio transmission. I would stand in my jeep or in the turret of my command tank facing the column and hold up my hand, arm bent at the elbow, palm out. That signal asked the question, "Are you ready?" Each tank commander would turn and use the same signal until the last tank was reached. The answer, "Ready," would come back the same way with the palm now facing forward. When it reached me, I would drop my hand, pump my fist, and the column would be moving. There were other signals for moving from a column into a line or for assembling on me to reform into a column.

One late afternoon we were moving down a two-lane asphalt road with rolling farmland on either side in a movement to contact with the opposing force. I was in the lead in my command tank when I spotted signs of an infantry position where the road disappeared over the next hill. Without really thinking about the maneuver damage, caught up in the exercise as I was, I gave the hand and arm signal to form a line. Without a hesitation, two tank platoons peeled off and came up on line on either side of me with the third platoon remaining in column in back of me, a move we had practiced countless times in our maneuver training. These movements were accomplished by adjusting speed so that the column made a fluid change without a halt into a line of eleven 5o-ton tanks sweeping up the hill toward the infantry position. The power of that line spread out at 1oo-yard intervals, moving forward at about 2o miles per hour, gave dramatic meaning to that old armor slogan about shock action. It is not a pleasant sight if you are hunkered down in a foxhole watching that amount of steel thunder toward you. The umpires stopped us before we overran the position, and there was only a minimum of comment about my having maneuvered through farm fields. At least it was late enough in the season that the crops had all been harvested. I never forgot that image of the power of properly trained armor moving in a coordinated way.

There was another lesson for me that came out of "Autumn Shield." Our commanding general, Major General John K. Waters, sent the division on an extended road march toward the end of the exercise that exceeded what anybody had expected—or planned for. The fuel available was what was available in the battalion's organic tanker trucks, and the road march soon exceeded the range of our tanks. One by one, my tanks dropped out along the road as they ran out of fuel. Eventually we reached our assigned *lager* for the night with four tanks and the wheeled vehicles. The other thirteen tanks were strung out behind us. We spent the night getting hot food back to the stranded tanks and getting fuel, as it became available, to them so they could rejoin us at our *lager*. It took the better part of the following day to reassemble, but again, the lesson of what happens when you exceed your supply line was indelibly impressed on my mind. Not a bad lesson for a division to learn in peacetime, and it had grown out of the World War II experience of some of our senior veteran tankers who had been through it with Patton's Third Army—when fuel had actually not been available.

Shortly after the end of "Autumn Shield," our battalion's turn came to exchange our gas guzzling M48's for the new M60 tanks. These tanks had a much more efficient engine, greater fuel capacity, and much greater range. They also were up gunned to a 105mm main gun, were much more user friendly, and had a far more accurate coincident range finder (much like the range finder on the Argus cameras of that time), though the super elevation was still added in mechanically by cams and linkage. The turn-in process was, however, all-consuming. To be accepted for turn in, the tanks had to be spotless and in absolutely ready condition. In addition, the so-called "on vehicle material" (OVM), which were all the spare parts and tools that were allocated to each tank, had to be accounted for. Either the individual items were present, were on order, or a survey of loss had to be initiated. Multiplied by the seventeen tanks in the company, it was an exercise in excruciating detail. After several weeks of intense effort, we got them loaded on to the German flatbed rail cars one last time, with fingers crossed that none of them would fail to be able to drive up onto the rail cars. Having a suddenly inoperable tank as it was about to be accepted for turn-in would have stopped the whole procedure. We breathed a huge sigh of relief as the loaded rail cars pulled out of our siding with all of our tanks.

This was not the last that I was to see of these tanks. Seven years later, and half a world away in Vietnam, I was to find some of these very tanks in the cavalry squadron of which I was then the executive officer. Some serial numbers just stick with you. By then, the tanks had been refitted with diesel engines and redesignated M48A3's. They ran, but they still had their idiosyncrasies. For one, the engine compartment was really too small to allow for good air circulation around the larger diesel engine, which led to overheating in the tropical climate of Vietnam. For another, sheer metal fatigue had started to set in, and the torsion bars that ran from a road wheel arm on one side to a socket on the other side, enabling the road wheels to move up and down to conform to uneven ground, had a habit of breaking under the middle of the tank. Extracting them and replacing them with a new one was a most unpleasant job, again made more difficult by the high temperatures. But they were still a more reliable tank for all their age and rough usage than the lightweight, flawed Sheridan (M551) that replaced them.

Not too long after we received our new M60 tanks, we had a chance to show them off to our German neighbors at McKee Barracks. The occasion was the annual German-American open house that was the culmination of German-American Friendship Week. It was a chance to build relationships with our German hosts and to show off our equipment. Refreshments were served, and the kids got to go for a ride in a tank or a jeep or a tank retriever. The *Bundeswehr* contingent from the depot on the other side of our airfield joined us in setting up equipment for the local people to see.

The German cargo trucks were amazingly high vehicles sitting on very large tires that gave them a huge amount of ground clearance. After puzzling over the high center of gravity of the trucks for a while, I asked one of the *Bundeswehr* noncommissioned officers why the trucks were so high and what the advantage was. Without a pause, he answered that we would need such vehicles on the steppes of Russia when we invaded. It should be remembered that at this point, most of the officers and noncommissioned officers in the *Bundeswehr* were veterans of the World War II *Wehrmact* and had little doubt about who was still the enemy. Again, it was a small moment, but it also left a lasting impression on me.

The M6o tanks were fast and reliable, which was a wonderful change from the old tanks that we had turned in. But in winter weather, they were almost too fast. If the driver was not careful—and sometimes even if he were—the tank would literally spin rubber. I had a scary introduction to that at Grafenwoehr just prior to our next major maneuver, "Wintershield." We had been at Grafenwoehr for a week or so brushing up on our maneuver tactics and march discipline prior to the start of "Wintershield." We were scheduled for a night march, but the weather had been cold and misty all day. As night fell, the temperature dropped, and it looked like a skim of ice was forming on the road surfaces. Battalion headquarters was undeterred by our report of the potential problem, and we were directed to conduct our night tactical march—which meant blackout conditions with only the little "cats eye" lights to mark the presence of a large tracked vehicle.

All started well, with us moving smoothly from our dispersed assembly area positions to a march column, crossing the "Initial Point" for the march right on time and lining out at the correct 100-yard interval. We moved along nicely, with me leading in my blacked-out jeep. Then we crested a hill and started down a long downhill. I could feel no problem under the jeep's wheel as my driver slowly descended in four-wheel drive and a low gear to the bridge that was the low point of the tank trail before it climbed back up on the other side. As we slowed for the bridge, I glanced back. To my horror, I could see glinting "cats eyes" pointing in every direction—including up—along the entire length of the downhill stretch.

I immediately stopped the column and radioed battalion to explain the problem. I then returned to work with the platoon leaders and the tank crews so that we could inch our 60-ton monsters back onto the tank trail from the high ground on either side. If the road had been elevated or if there has been steep borrows on either side of the road, the tanks would have slid off the road and run the danger of tipping or throwing a track at the extreme angles that would have been encountered. As luck would have it, the terrain on either side was higher than the road. The tanks simply slid uphill until gravity stopped them, leaving them at all angles, but with no serious damage or crew injury. We spent the next couple of hours carefully moving the tanks to the bottom of the slope and then continued on to our base camp. The uphills were no problem as the tank tracks crunched the skim ice, but the weight of the tank combined with the use of brakes on the downhill had initiated the slides. I breathed a sigh of relief when we closed into our motor pool for the night.

During this same stay at Grafenwoehr, I had another run-in with weather. We were out training in one of the maneuver areas when a whiteout suddenly blanketed our company position. There was snow on the ground, and it had been foggy, but now we could see nothing. The radio told me that the battalion commander and the battalion operations officer (S3) were on the nearby tank trail looking for us, but they could not see us. Using my map and a compass, I made my way very slowly to the tank trail. Despite the snail's pace of my progress, I only covered about 200 meters before emerging out of the fog bank on the edge of the trail, which was relatively visible because there was no snow cover on it to blend into the fog. Close by were the jeeps carrying my battalion commander and our S3.

They could not believe that a whole tank company had been covered up by the fog just off the tank trail and thought that I had gotten disoriented and taken the company out of our assigned training area. Having assured them that we were where we were supposed to be, I disappeared back into the fog. There is nothing quite as scary as hearing tanks moving but not being able to see them—and then having the barrels of the main tank guns poke through the fog very close to you! And that would be the kind of battle that we might have been involved in if the Soviets had ever come through those narrow German valleys up by the interzonal border in winter. Tank engagements would have been at no more than 500 meters.

The maneuver that followed demonstrated how hard it is to outguess nature. The weather continued cold, with freezing rain and snow. The 2nd Armored Cavalry Regiment had therefore taken the initiative to reverse every second center guide on both tracks of each of their tanks. The center guide was a steel U-shaped piece in the center of each track block that kept the track on-line as it passed around the drive sprocket and over the suspension rollers. To accomplish the reversal so that every other U-shaped guide faced out (the legs of the "U" were about four inches long) had taken an enormous effort—each track had to be broken and laid out flat, and every second center guide had to be loosened and turned 180 degrees. It worked to keep the tanks from sliding initially, but then we had a thaw, and the ice and the frozen snowpack melted, leaving bare asphalt for the tanks with their spiked tracks to eat into. Of course, the pace of the maneuver prohibited the unit taking the time to turn the center guides back to their proper alignment facing in. I had seen the road between Hohenfels and Parsberg as the maneuver got under way because our initial position was on the edge of the Hohenfels training area where the highway turned at the border of the reservation. I saw it again as we moved to the railhead at Parsberg to load our tanks for the trip back to McKee Barracks. The road looked just like a pasture that a very large herd of cattle had stirred to a muddy morass.

I was back in the area in later years and marveled at the three-lane road, with turn islands at the intersections that had replaced the original, perfectly serviceable road. I suppose somebody would be held accountable these days, but it was simply maneuver damage in those days, and we paid for the new road—and more than a few chickens that had also gotten in the way.

By the time of "Wintershield," we had a new commanding general, Major General James K. Polk, who would later be the Command in Chief of U.S. Army Europe. He had been the "eyes and ears" of Patton's Third Army during World War II and was a professional cavalry and armor officer. Watching him drop into the tank commander's position on a tank when he visited our unit made you understand very quickly that this was a general who knew tanks—and you had better know what you were doing too.

Like General Waters, General Polk also took advantage of our major exercises, such as "Wintershield," to conduct some additional training. His approach was to surprise the division by prolonging the major exercise by a day or two and purposely driving us off the maps that we carried. His point, based on his experience in World War II, was that you had to be prepared to not only outrun your supply line, but your maps. There was invariably a rush to buy German road maps at gas stations that we passed, and we learned that it paid to be familiar with the terrain and road network in your entire sector of responsibility and well beyond. Again, the lesson was a good one, and one that stuck with me over the years. I formed the habit of accumulating map sheets for the areas bordering my assigned area of operation and usually found a large-scale aviation chart that showed the road network for a much larger area, including all of Vietnam south of the demilitarized zone during my time there.

9

THE BORDER AND THE BERLIN WALL

When I arrived in Germany in February 1960, the interzonal border between East and West Germany was unevenly marked by old stone border markers that looked remarkably like gravestones. The East German side had a 10-meter plowed strip of dirt reaching back to the east from those markers. The *Grenztruppen* (East German Border Troops), who patrolled this plowed strip, were a surly bunch who operated in pairs. They used the plowed strip to detect any footprints of border crossers. A favorite prank of one noncommissioned officer from the 14th Cavalry Regiment, which patrolled the northernmost sector of the border, was to walk backwards across the ploughed strip, which left footprints for the *Grenztruppen* to puzzle over. The *Grenztruppen* would counter by hiding in a handy clump of bushes to try to catch unwary East Germans trying to escape west — or some of our more adventurous cavalry troopers who would cross over in some deserted area to "count coup" by peeing on East German soil.

Within the two-kilometer zone on the West German side, the *Bundesgrenzeshutz* (the West German Border Guards) and their dogs patrolled. There were warning signs stating, "*HALT – ZONENGRENZE*" at the two-kilometer and 50-meter point, where all roads leading to the border were blocked by simple steel barriers, but that was about it. At that time, there were no additional fences, no towers, no mines, no nothing!

With all the rural secondary roads between East and West Germany blocked, and armed guards manning the few authorized crossing points, cross border traffic was very light. The bridges on many of the secondary roads had been destroyed and the trickle of legal traffic across the border was channeled over a few easily controlled main roads and the *autobahn* crossing point at Helmstedt, which led to the Berlin corridor through which we had treaty rights for ground transit into Berlin. The railroads, except for the line that ran inside the Berlin corridor, had also been cut at the border, some so suddenly that the train cars were halted in place and would remain stopped on the tracks for some forty years.

The one soft spot in this dangerous, if somewhat vague, barrier to escape from East Germany was Berlin. There, no plowed strip was possible and patrolling the divide was difficult and cumbersome. A person could take a one-way trip from East to West on the underground (reconstructed *U-bahn* or *S-bahn*) and disappear into West Germany. That all changed in the early morning hours of Sunday, August 13, 1961, when the initial pieces of what would become the Berlin Wall went up. That first provisional barrier was improved and thickened over time to become a formidable obstacle for any Easterner wanting to escape to the West.

The Potsdam Convention (1945) had divided Berlin into four occupation zones (American, British, French, and Soviet) under a joint command. Mounting tension between the Western allies and Russia led to Russia withdrawing from this joint command in 1948. Berlin then became a split city with the American, British, and French zones becoming West Berlin and the Soviet zone becoming East Berlin. In 1949, West Berlin became a member state of the Federal Republic of Germany, while the Soviet sector of Berlin became the capital of the East German Democratic Republic. The Russians used the introduction of West German currency into West Berlin as the reason for the Berlin Blockade in 1948 and 1949, which resulted in the storied Berlin Airlift. Minor incidents continued after that crisis subsided, and in 1958, Khrushchev demanded the withdrawal of Western troops and an end to the occupation status of Berlin. Negotiations continued on this issue through 1960 without any progress.

In the meantime, the flow of East Germans to West Germany continued unabated in Berlin since there was no significant border barrier between East and West Berlin. An East German could simply get on the *U-bahn* or *S-bahn* at a station in East Berlin and come up at a station in West Berlin. Between January and August of 1961, over 160,000 refugees fled across the border in Berlin. In order to staunch this flow, which consisted in the main of the most intelligent and productive members of their population, the East German regime began the erection of the Berlin "anti-fascist protection wall" on that Sunday morning in August. At the first signs of the wall construction, USAREUR went on full alert with all of its combat units moving to their dispersal areas. Nobody at that moment knew the full intent of the East German government and their Soviet masters.

President Kennedy sent retired General Lucius Clay (who had been Military Governor of the U.S. Zone of Occupation and was much respected by the Berliners) as a special advisor with the rank of ambassador to Berlin, along with Vice President Lyndon Johnson. They arrived on Saturday, August 19. Meanwhile, the 1st Battle Group, 18th Infantry, from the 8th Infantry Division, was alerted to march over the *autobahn* to Berlin to test Soviet intentions and to assert our treaty rights to the Berlin corridor through which the *autobahn* ran to Berlin. We all held our breath to see if the 18th Infantry would be opposed as they traversed the Berlin corridor across East Germany to Berlin. They were not, of course, and instead were met by crowds of cheering Berliners throwing flowers at their vehicles. The Vice President addressed the crowds and assured the audience that the United States would defend them. The Cold War, however, heated up considerably as the previously porous Berlin border was turned into the most conspicuous piece of a continuously improved Iron Curtain, along which some kind of conflict was to be a daily occurrence for the next thirty years.

We tend to forget how tense that period was after the Wall went up. When we moved to our dispersal areas, fully loaded with our basic load of ammunition for all our weapons, we knew that if the 18th Infantry were opposed, we would move to our general alert positions to prepare for war with the Soviets. One of my Air Force classmates captured the tension perfectly. He had been on a short vacation and had stopped at Hahn Air Base on the way back to his air base in France. As he and his wife drove through the gate, the guard told him that "the balloon had already gone up." He drove on through the gate and over to another classmate's quarters and then on to the Officers Club, which was doing a grand business. The F-105s at Hahn were armed with nuclear weapons and "everything that could fly was armed, cocked, and aimed east." The Club was doing great business while the pilots waited for the word that never came because the conventional wisdom was that the missions were one-way missions!

The dispatch of that 1st Battle Group, 18th Infantry has a wonderful story of its own that is known to very few. All that the world knew from the press reports was that an infantry battle group road marched to Berlin as a show of force and to test the intentions of the Soviets, that in the end it was unopposed, and that life went on with the added obstacle of a real Iron Curtain dividing Berlin and the boundary between East and West. There is, however, the rest of the story.

I heard the first part of it within a year from a West Point classmate who was the junior aide to Lieutenant General Gar Davidson, the commander of the Seventh Army and the former Superintendent of the Military Academy during much of our time as cadets. The Seventh Army was the combat component of U.S. Army Europe at that time, and the 8th Infantry Division and its 1st Battle Group,

18th Infantry belonged to the Seventh Army. In point of fact, there was another headquarters, the V Corps, between the Seventh Army and the 8th Infantry Division. General Davidson's first knowledge that one of his infantry battle groups was on the move to Berlin and to a potential armed confrontation with the Russians came from the morning news on the Armed Forces Radio Network. We chortled over that because the USAREUR commander at the time, General Bruce C. Clarke, was a prolific writer on proper leadership techniques. However, he had, in this case, apparently reached down to the battle group commander, Colonel Glover Johns, without a by your leave to the three intermediate commanders (the Seventh Army commanding general, the V Corps commanding general, and the 8th Infantry Division commanding general). He dispatched the unit into what could well have been the start of World War III without immediately notifying any of them.

There is some dispute as to who handpicked Colonel Johns to lead the reinforcement column, but it is clear that either President John F. Kennedy himself or General Bruce Clark personally selected him. Colonel Johns was a much-decorated World War II veteran who had once served as General George Patton's aide and was later to be the technical advisor on the film *Patton*. He was a soldier's soldier who still carried an old fashioned .45 revolver as his personal sidearm. Whichever senior leader selected Johns, they certainly had the right man for the mission.

Over the years, I have found that there was a lot more to the story than I knew at the time, and many years later I got an even fuller account from another classmate who had been the aide to the 8th Infantry Division's commanding general back then.

In August 1961, the 8th Infantry Division was headquartered at Bad Kreuznach with major units stationed there, near Heidelberg at Mannheim, at Mainz, and at Baumholder. On the weekend that the 1st Battle Group, 18th Infantry was alerted to march to Berlin, however, most of the division's infantry battle groups were not present at these home stations for one reason or another. The 1st Battle Group, 16th Infantry, was at Normandy acting as background extras for the filming of *The Longest Day*. Much of the remainder of the division was at Sennelager in northern Germany doing field training at that British Major Training Area. The 1st Battle Group, 26th Infantry was acting as the aggressor force on the ground at Sennelager and one of the airborne battle groups had jumped in to oppose them, with the second airborne battle group to follow. The 1st Battle Group, 18th Infantry was at its home station at Sandhofen, just outside of Mannheim, but all of its company commanders and their radio jeeps were also at Sennelager acting as controllers for the opposing forces exercise in progress there, a fact of which higher headquarters was apparently unaware. The division commander had also gone north to Sennelager that weekend to watch the exercise.

Sometime during the late afternoon of Saturday, August 19, the division's headquarters started to get inquiries from its next higher headquarters, V Corps, regarding radio communications that they had picked up that were associated with the 18th Infantry's call signs. Corps headquarters wanted to know what was going on, but nobody at division headquarters at Bad Kreuznach knew. The Corps G3 then called the 8th Division's exercise command post at Sennelager looking for the commanding general, who was out visiting the units involved in the training exercise. By late evening, under mounting pressure from V Corps, the duty officer at the exercise command post eventually woke the division chief of staff, Colonel Jack Wright, who had more insight into contingency planning than others because of his position. He guessed that it must be about Berlin.

Eventually, Major General Edgar C. Doleman, the division commander, was brought back to the exercise command post and a priority top secret "flash" message—which the division duty officer at Bad Kreuznach had thought to merely be part of the exercise play—was brought forward, along with the cryptographic keys and ciphers that enabled the exercise command post to read the encoded traffic. It was then that they learned that the 18th Infantry was to depart Coleman Barracks outside of Mannheim the following morning to road march to Berlin.

The delivery of the top-secret "flash" message and the cryptographic keys and ciphers is a side story of its own. The officer in charge of the division's communications center, another West Point classmate of mine, dropped by the center that Saturday to make sure all was well. Outside the center, he was approached by a general from USAREUR headquarters who asked where the division commanding general was. After explaining that the general was in the field, the lieutenant became involved with tracking down the message traffic regarding Berlin. He found that the division duty officer had received a hard copy of a decoded classified "flash" message directing the 18th Infantry to move to Berlin, but had thought it was part of the exercise play up north. The USAREUR general demanded that my classmate fly the message and the cryptographic keys and ciphers to the division commander's location. My classmate properly pointed out that regulations prohibited coded messages and the cryptographic keys and ciphers used to decode the message from being transported together in the same plane. The general told him to just do it!

So, my classmate took the classified material to the airfield and found a second lieutenant pilot and an aircraft. Since my classmate was himself a rated aviator, he tracked the route the aircraft was flying rather more closely than some passengers might and soon realized that they were headed for the interzonal border with East Germany. He eventually convinced the young, inexperienced pilot that he was headed into trouble—the inexperienced lieutenant was tuned in to a bogus decoy beacon meant to lure aircraft into East German airspace, a ploy that actually worked years later on the

Turkish-Russian border—and got him turned around and landed at Sennelager.

The next challenge was getting the 18th Infantry's company commanders and their radio jeeps, which were still in the exercise area, back to Mannheim in time for the early morning departure the following day. A helicopter unit was contacted that flew medium- lift H-37 helicopters capable of transporting the company commanders and their radio jeeps. It was, however, a dark, rainy night, and the aviation folks remonstrated about flying a "training" mission in such weather. They were convinced that there was actually a mission-essential need and initiated planning for what would be the first operational instrument-flight-rules flight for H-37 aircraft in Germany. The effort was successful, and the company commanders and their critical radio jeeps arrived at the airfield at Coleman Barracks outside of Mannheim about thirty minutes before the scheduled departure of their battle group.

The battle group marched up the *autobahn* that Sunday morning toward the junction at Kassel, where the *autobahn* that runs east to Berlin through the Berlin corridor joins the main north-south West German *autobahn*. The column of 490 military vehicles was stretched over some fifty miles and interspersed with German civilian traffic because it was still an administrative road march despite the potential for a confrontation with the Soviets that might lead to war. In that confusion, the fuel tankers had fallen to the end of the battle group column instead of accompanying their companies. By the time the column reached Kassel, it was hungry for fuel.

General Doleman had flown into Kassel by this time for a final consultation with Colonel Johns and other senior officers before the battle group headed east into the unknown of the Berlin corridor. Realizing the fuel problem, he commandeered the European Exchange System (EES) gas station located near the *autobahn* junction and ordered the German manager to start filling the military vehicles as they pulled off the *autobahn*. One can only guess at the manager's anxiety level as the gallons of gasoline meant for privately owned vehicles were poured into the hungry military vehicles and the pump meters clicked off the cost even at the reduced EES price of twenty-one cents a gallon, twenty-three for high test. The battle group's fuel tankers eventually caught up and finished the refueling process before the EES gas station was run completely dry.

The march to Berlin was tense but uneventful for the battle group. The East German VOPOs lined the route and East German military units over watched the march column, but the only hold up occurred as the *autobahn* ended and the column crossed into the Soviet sector from East Germany on its way to the American sector. The Soviet authorities demanded a head count of every occupant of every vehicle. After a lot of discussion, Colonel Johns eventually gave in and dismounted his troops from their vehicles while the Soviets counted each soldier. The process took almost three hours. In the meantime, a nervous Vice President Lyndon Johnson and retired General Lucius Clay were kept waiting at the Dreilindern Gate, the entrance to the American sector, where they had come to welcome the relief column. Years later, Colonel Johns said that it was one of the most humiliating moments of his career. For a time, battle groups were rotated in and out of Berlin every three months to assert American treaty rights and to augment the Berlin Brigade to make an appropriate show of force.

What began in Berlin on that Sunday morning in August eventually became a heavily fortified and fairly impenetrable interzonal border that divided West Germany from East Germany and Czechoslovakia. What had been a vaguely marked border between the East and the West evolved into a very inhospitable demarcation line. By the following summer, a minefield, anti-tank obstacles, and wooden watchtowers had augmented the 10-meter plowed strip on the eastern side of the border. The

East German Border Troops, well trained and equipped with modern light infantry weapons, patrolled this newly strengthened border around the clock, ruthlessly enforcing rigid travel control measures. Over the next ten years, the minefields were made more dense, high voltage electrified wire fences were installed, concrete and steel guard towers replaced the original wood structures, and trip flares and booby traps sprouted along the length of the interzonal border creating a wide no man's land reaching back some distance to the east.

Though much less publicized than the Berlin Wall, the most poignant example of the newly fortified interzonal border was the section that neatly divided a small West German farm town in half. From the air, the new Iron Curtain could be seen to run down the main street of the tiny village from one end to the other. One could only imagine the personal impact on the villagers who could literally look across the street into forbidden territory where they had previously been welcomed by their across-the-street neighbors or relatives.

Though the world rarely heard of it, there would be confrontations of some sort along this upgraded armed border on an almost daily basis. For instance, early in the fall of 1961, the East German Border Troops sought to intimidate the West German farmers whose fields abutted the newly strengthened border by taking pot shots at them from their wood guard towers as they tried to harvest their sugar beets. Our response was to move tanks to the edge of the fields facing east toward the border so that pot shots would be aimed at our tanks as well as the working farmers. The shooting stopped! Years later, when the Vietnam War had turned some of the more liberal German population against America, we could still count on an enthusiastic welcome up by the border whenever our tanks passed through the farm villages up there.

The border was patrolled in different ways by the different armored cavalry regiments, depending on the distance from the border of their respective home stations in their respective sectors. The 14th Armored Cavalry Regiment's (later reflagged after Vietnam as the 11th Armored Cavalry Regiment) squadrons were stationed in *kasernes* at Bad Hersfeld, Fulda, and Bad Kissingen, which were all fairly close to the border in this northernmost sector, so it sent its cavalry troops out to patrol and man their observation posts from those home stations. The 2nd Armored Cavalry Regiment's squadrons were located at Bindlach, just outside of Bayreuth; Bamberg; and Amberg; which were a good distance from the border because of the way it jutted to the east in that middle sector. As a result, it sent its cavalry troops to border camps for a month at a time and the troops patrolled and manned their observation posts from those border camps. The 11th Armored Cavalry Regiment (located at Regensberg, Straubing, and Landshut before it gave up its responsibility to the West German Border Guards) performed its border mission using a combination of the approaches used by its two sister regiments because of the varying distances of its squadron's home stations from the border. To the north of the 14th Armored Cavalry Regiment, the British were responsible for the border as it wended its way to the Baltic Sea.

Regardless of where the troops were located for their border duty, the cavalry regiments maintained a 24-hour-a-day, seven-day-a-week vigilance along the entire length of the border within the American zone of responsibility. The scout sections of the troops pulling border duty patrolled in their ¼ ton machinegun-mounted jeeps while the remainder of the troop (tank sections, infantry squads, and mortar squads) manned observation posts or were on standby in case the scouts encountered a situation that required that they be reinforced. The soldiers and officers serving in these regiments spent even more time in the field than the divisional units because they still had the usual gunnery qualification, tactical training, and annual proficiency testing that the divisional units had in addition to their regular border responsibilities. When they went for this training or testing, one of the divisional cavalry squadrons filled in for them on the border.

The erection of the Berlin Wall resulted in an increase in troop strength for USAREUR and for the U.S. Army as a whole, though the Eisenhower administration had been in the process of drawing down that strength prior to the Wall. In the late 1950s, the U.S. Army had been at its lowest strength since the Korean War, and there seemed to be no reason to believe that much would change in that status when I was commissioned in 1958.

In the late winter and early spring of 1961, officers and noncommissioned officers were being curtailed—rotated to assignments in the United States or elsewhere short of the standard three-year tour in Europe. Now, these same people found themselves on orders back to USAREUR as we brought our units to full strength to face any eventuality. Funding also increased, and limitations on tracked-vehicle movement that had been based on a shortage of funding for fuel and repair parts were lifted. The Army was expanding, the sense of urgency in USAREUR increasing, and the pace of activities was picking up because the Berlin Wall had demonstrated that our confrontation with the East was not going to go away. We could not know at that time that Vietnam would ensure a continued expansion of the Army, while the pace would become absolutely frenetic.

And so the border, which was continually being strengthened and thickened on the east side after the Berlin Wall went up, became the focus of the U.S. Army in Europe. It was patrolled for the next twenty-eight years, and a potential attack across it became the basis for all of the Army's war plans, while its looming guard towers over watching from its east side became a symbol of the Cold War. Shots were exchanged sporadically across this border, and border incidents were an almost daily occurrence. What is still not widely recognized is the relentless pressure on the troops who patrolled that border and were to be the tripwire if there was going to be an attack from the east. The cavalry regiments would have to delay the enemy long enough to enable their families to evacuate their forward *kasernes* and the four divisions behind them to come up to occupy their initial forward general alert positions. Those divisions would then have to delay the enemy long enough to enable reinforcements to start streaming in from the United States. Those responsibilities weighed heavily on commanders at all levels and provided a motivation for the units that was simply not central to service on the large posts in the United States. There was always a sense of urgency in those early years after the Berlin Wall went up that is hard to grasp at this distance in time.

10

THE LIFE

The erection of the Berlin Wall and the hardening of the barriers on the interzonal border that accompanied that action had minimal impact on our day-to-day military routine. An immediate and dramatic impact on our social activities, however, was a curfew imposed by the USAREUR Commander in Chief, General Bruce Clark. All officers, noncommissioned officers, and enlisted men were directed to be in barracks or quarters by midnight. The goal was a well-rested, ready force. The reality was that it just made it more difficult for married officers and noncommissioned officers to engage in a normal social life, though it did cut into the bar hopping of the single officer, noncommissioned officer, and enlisted population as intended. Fortunately, at least in our case, it was not hard to evade the curfew because our quarters were outside the McKee Barracks fences; therefore, it was unnecessary to pass by the military police manning the gate to get to our quarters. If you were involved in an accident or an incident, you would be in trouble; if you were simply going from one set of quarters to another, it was a pretty safe gamble.

Not so safe was driving to an Ella Fitzgerald concert in Munich—a three-hour drive at best. Ella Fitzgerald was a singing legend, and we very much wanted to take the opportunity to hear her in person. Getting down to the concert was not a problem, but we talked at length about how to gett out of Munich after the concert without getting stopped. We had already purchased the tickets (at a cost of twelve deutsche mark each, or about $3.00 apiece) before the curfew was announced. We really wanted to hear her sing in person, so we and another couple drove to Munich on the appointed Saturday afternoon. Driving down in the afternoon was no problem, of course, but the concert didn't end until about 10:30 p.m. That was a problem, but we managed to escape Munich with our U.S. Forces license plates before the witching hour. We then drove home very carefully on the back roads and *autobahn*, where encountering our military police was unlikely, and rolled into the parking space in front of our apartment building very quietly.

The only other time I took a chance on the curfew, aside from going between quarters, was to attend the annual celebration of the founding of the U.S. Military Academy. Stuttgart was the closest central location for this formal gathering, held annually around the world, and we carpooled down. Since our battalion commander, Major (promotable) Dale Crittenberger, was also a graduate and was with us, we believed that we probably would escape any adverse results because of his presence and the august nature of the occasion. Still, we were very careful on the drive home—and none of us brought up the subject of the curfew.

Another, less benign, but more restricted result of the heightened confrontational nature of the border was an elevating of the tensions regarding the liaison missions. The Soviets and Americans had established reciprocal liaison missions early on, theirs based in Frankfurt and ours based in Potsdam, a suburb of East Berlin. The increased tensions between East and West caused the respective missions to become overt espionage operations instead of coordination missions. While both Russians and Americans recognized the right of the other mission to travel in their respective sectors, each also marked-off restricted areas in which mission travel was prohibited. These areas, typically maneuver areas or military bases, were like a magnet for the mission personnel on both sides, who were trying to keep up to date on troop strengths, troop unit stationing, new developments in weapons and equipment, and newly developed tactics.

The result was a game in which each mission tried to penetrate the other's restricted areas without being caught. We were prohibited from using force to corral the Soviet liaison mission if we found them in our restricted areas. All we could do was use our vehicles to block them in and call for the military police to escort them out of the restricted area. All USAREUR military personnel were issued a card listing the proper protocol to be used if they encountered a Soviet liaison mission vehicle in a restricted area (these restricted areas were clearly outlined on our maps), and the penalty for not following the protocol was heavy. As you might imagine, the Soviets were far less reluctant to use force on our people when they were found in a restricted area, and injuries and damage to our vehicles were not uncommon in East Germany. In fact, in the 1970s, a major from our mission was killed over there by Soviet troops who found him where they thought he ought not to be.

Travel to Berlin for non-duty visits had always been restricted. It was possible to drive the *autobahn* in the Berlin corridor to Berlin, but there was always a risk of a breakdown, a wrong turn, or being stopped for speeding whether you were or not. Those of us with high security clearances were simply not allowed to take that chance. The alternative was to fly, which was expensive even in those days given the size of our salaries, or take the "Duty Train." One of these trains departed Frankfurt on a daily basis in the early morning to carry replacements and cargo to Berlin, and a similar train departed Berlin in the late afternoon each day for the overnight return to Frankfurt. It was possible to reserve a compartment on these trains for non-duty travel for the whole family, and over the years we took advantage of the opportunity.

Travel on the Duty Train required obtaining travel authorization in advance in the form of "flag orders," so called because the authorization, written in both English and Russian, had a full-color American flag printed at the top of the authorization order sheet. The order authorized travel from the border crossing point at Helmstedt to Berlin and back. Once settled in your compartment on the train, the orders were collected by the military police contingent that rode the train. The train would stop on the outskirts of Berlin at the entrance to the Soviet sector inside a cyclone fence that ran the length of the train on either side of the track. The military police would take the collected flag orders and go outside the fence to meet with their Russian counterparts. This formality was conducted for every train passage, going and coming, but rarely was there an incident. It was a routine that allowed the Russian side to exert their authority without allowing them to infringe on the treaty-guaranteed right of transit represented by the railroad right of way inside the fence.

There was a small L-shaped guardhouse for the Russian soldiers just outside the cyclone fence. One evening , we were returning from Berlin during a subsequent tour of duty in Germany in the early 1970s, and we watched the scripted dance of the two guard contingents verifying the flag orders. The procedure completed, the train started to move and the Russian guards paced back to their guardhouse. They had just reached the inset of the L as we watched out the compartment window, backlit by our compartment's lights. The two Russian soldiers, submachine guns cradled across their chests, looked up at us, and one of them gave the "V" peace sign that was so common in that era. Apparently junior enlisted men have similar outlooks in all armies.

On that later trip to Berlin, we visited a good friend who had previously served on the interzonal border in the 14th Armored Cavalry Regiment, and who had then gone on to earn his advanced degree in Russian. We had taught at the Military Academy at the same time, he teaching Russian and me teaching English to the cadets, before moving on separately to Vietnam and then back to Europe, where he was now a member of our liaison mission. He lived in Berlin with his family, but he did his duty tours driving through East Germany from the Potsdam mission compound. On this visit between our families, he had arranged for me to join him at the mission on a day when he was simply performing administrative duties in his office in the Potsdam compound.

Early in the morning on the designated day, we drove across the Havel River on the storied Glienicke Bridge—the same bridge over which U2 pilot Gary Powers and other covert detainees were exchanged from time to time—into East Berlin in a souped-up, olive drab Ford whose only identification were American flag license plates on the front and back bumpers. We were, of course, both in full Army Green uniform. We stopped at the checkpoint at the western-sector end of the bridge to submit our papers (and be surreptitiously photographed by a hidden camera that my friend had warned me about) and then drove across the bridge toward the Russian soldiers standing guard at the East German end. We apparently arrived more quickly than expected because a Russian officer was still adjusting the coat of the guard so that he would look just right for the passing Americans. The coat, I might add, was an exact replica of the design and color that had been used in the czarist armies. Go figure!

The drive to the mission compound was interesting. It was a dull, grey German morning with heavy mist still hanging in the air at that early hour. I felt as though I had landed in a black and white movie about World War II. Potsdam had been heavily damaged in the war, and the repair had been marginal even after all the time that had elapsed. The walls of some buildings were still clearly shell pocked, and the only source of light in each shop was a single bare light bulb hanging from a single wire in the center of the ceiling. The contrast with the modern neon and fluorescent lighting common to commercial facilities in West Germany was dramatic. There were also a lot of uniforms in evidence — postal workers, street cleaners, and many others seemed to all be dressed in drab unornamented uniforms of one kind or another. What were incongruous in the extreme were the surreptitious "V" signs that were flashed at us when these uniformed civilian pedestrians saw the American flag on our bumper.

The mission compound itself was situated on the edge of a lake on the outskirts of Potsdam. A fence enclosed it, and the entrance gate was locked and guarded. I spent the day wandering inside the compound fence while my friend worked. We came together for a good German lunch, and then I went back to wandering and taking pictures of the outside on a day when the light on the marsh edging the lake reminded me very much of the misty, yellowish light used to film the movie *Dr. Zhivago*. As I was composing one of my pictures, the East German female cook, who had prepared our noon meal, left the mission building, headed home at the end of her workday. She noticed me taking pictures and carefully placed a tree between her and me. I moved to the right, and she moved to the left. It soon became obvious that she did not want her picture taken! Apparently electronic bugging was not the only way the Soviets kept track of what was going on in the mission. Both sides, of course, knew of those efforts and acted accordingly.

This visit to Berlin, which occurred in the early 1970s, had an interesting impact on my oldest daughter. Julie was a pre-teenager and it was the Vietnam era, so she had naturally absorbed a certain amount of the propaganda about our misunderstanding the Eastern Bloc countries and their Soviet overseers. That made for some interesting dinner-table discussions. As part of this visit to Berlin, we went to the famous Checkpoint Charlie and several other tourist observation points that had been set up to view what had become the very substantial wall that divided the city. From one of those observation points, we could see a number of memorial markers commemorating where East Germans had been killed trying to get over the wall. Julie asked what they were, and we explained to her that they marked the spot where civilians had been killed simply for trying to cross the border. Thereafter, she was somewhat more skeptical of the appeasement propaganda that was in circulation. Those markers had a profound impact on everybody who saw them, bringing home the undeniable cruelty and repression of the regimes across the wall.

Until the early 1970s, the U.S. Army worked a five-and-a-half-day week. That did not stop us from celebrating the end of the work week on Friday night for "Happy Hour" at the Officers Club—since Saturday morning was usually given over to administrative work and inspections of barracks and personal and unit equipment. Social life on small posts like McKee Barracks centered on the Club, and our wives would join us toward the end of Happy Hour for dinner and socializing. Though Happy Hour prices made these occasions possible on our slim disposable incomes, the Clubs were eminently affordable all the time because of the support that came from the omnipresent slot machines. The profits from these machines underwrote the whole club system: officer, noncommissioned officer, and enlisted. One of the Officer of the Day routine duties was to supervise the emptying of the "slots" and the accounting for the money turned in to a local depository for transfer to the club system's headquarters. Some years later, reformers concerned about gambling addiction and the resulting impact on the low family incomes eliminated the slot machines from all clubs, and the club system fell into disrepair. Prices went up, quality went down, and consolidation of the respective rank-specific clubs was not uncommon, particularly at the smaller posts. The result was an entirely different ambiance and a loss of comradery.

One of the unfortunate aspects of Friday night Happy Hours was the rite of initiation that took place in many units. A new officer, with his wife as witness if concurrent travel had been granted, was introduced to the unit at these Happy Hours, which frequently served the additional function of a "Hail and Farewell" event. As part of the rite of initiation, the new officer would be asked (pressured) into "chugging" a one-liter glass boot of beer. The results were predictable and embarrassing. In later years, when I became a more senior commander, I eliminated this "tradition" because it was simply an imposition on the new officer and his wife to have to undergo it in front of his new unit after having just completed a sleepless flight and ground trip to their new post from the States.

The Club was also a major venue for the Officers Wives Clubs that actively existed on every post, big or small. On the small *kasernes*, it was a major support system for the wives during the extended absences of their husbands on field training exercises or during Major Training Area stints. It sponsored luncheons, bridge parties, bowling outings at the local bowling alley, if there was one, and major fund raiser parties for a number of post activities such as a lending closet for new arrivals, a child care facility, the Army Community Service, and the like. While many of these events took place at the Club, there were also smaller club-sponsored events in the respective quarters of the members.

My wife, who was never a bowler, created one of those memorable bowling party events that every family's kids hear about for years. The local bowling alley was located in the last row of buildings before the motor pools took over across the street. It also was right next to the enlisted men's club. Since the bowling alley had soda machines, it was a magnet for junior enlisted soldiers on break from pulling maintenance on their tracked vehicles. The presence of women in the bowling alley during Wives Club-sponsored bowling was an added attraction for the spectators, who were inclined to linger lined up behind the alleys. On one such occasion, my wife, who had perfected the "backward release," pretty well cleared out the lounging soldiers by accidently releasing the bowling ball as she brought it to the rear. Suddenly the motor pool seemed like a safer option to the spectators.

It was a very social Army when the men were not in the field, with small groups gathering in quarters of a Saturday evening or going out to sample the food at the many local *gasthauses* in the area. Again, the very favorable rate of exchange at the time made it very affordable to go out for dinner with wine or beer, so it was not unusual for couples to go out for dinner alone or with others. Hard liquor was rare and very expensive at these local eateries, so being over served was rarely a problem. In fact, social drinking at parties in quarters could be more dangerous. In keeping with the times, drinks would be served before dinner, wine would be served with dinner, and after-dinner drinks were usual. Fortunately, returning to your own quarters did not involve driving and was typically only a stairwell or two away. It must be remembered that these were the years when there was no social pressure against smoking or drinking. Even alcoholism was tolerated in the Army of the time, unless it led to inappropriate conduct.

Since there was always a large population of bachelor officers, particularly among the lieutenant ranks, there was a perennial shortage of single women, just as there had been on the small western posts of the Indian-fighting Army of the later 1800s. The advent of the Department of Defense school system and the Service Club System to support off-duty activities for the enlisted ranks gave some relief since both organizations were overwhelmingly staffed by single women. The result was a happy social life for singles and a good many marriages. Meeting German women was somewhat more challenging because of language differences and because single German women at that time did not go to *gasthuases* on their own. Still, there were a good number of German brides during this period, though the administrative obstacles were still formidable, including permission to marry from your commander.

A responsibility that belonged to bachelor officers and couples without children at that time had to do with holiday duty. By tradition, officers with children were exempted from Officer of the Day duty and Officer of the Guard duty on family holidays such as Thanksgiving, Christmas, or Easter. It was a responsibility that was gladly fulfilled in order to improve the quality of family life, and single officers or couples without children could always eat in the mess hall on those special occasions with their celebratory Army mess hall meals.

In the end, we would spend ten years of our Army service in West Germany with two other tours added to this initial one. In that time, we watched West Germany become a prosperous country that became increasingly expensive for Americans stationed there. But on that first tour, the rate of exchange was 4.2 deutsche marks to the dollar when we arrived, and even lieutenants could afford to take advantage of all that West Germany had to offer. We ate out in the welcoming *gasthauses* frequently, and we purchased traditional German clothing that matched the cool, wet climate. Nobody left Germany without a loden coat and other distinctive and warm boiled wool jackets and sweaters. Some collected clocks of all sorts, and others collected *Drillings*: three-barreled hunting weapons that were some combination of rifle and shotgun barrels and had emerged from where they had been hidden during the war. There were also Rod and Gun Clubs on every little *kaserne* where weapons could be purchased tax-free and where there were facilities for off-duty shooting.

The rate of exchange was so favorable that it tempted us to buy a Mercedes-Benz sedan midway through that first tour. The going price for a six-cylinder 220S four-door sedan was the equivalent of $3,200. When a lieutenant, freshly assigned from the States, moved into our stairwell with his brand-new Chevrolet Impala four-door sedan, huge fins and all, and I discovered that he had paid $3,300 for it, our minds were made up. We sold our 1954 Ford convertible that had served us so well and purchased our first new car: a graphite gray Mercedes 220S. We drove that car for ten years and broke even when we sold it back in the United States. The Ford did not do as well. The new owner smashed it into the concrete side of a narrow bridge within months of purchasing it. Fortunately, I had been paid in full before that event.

Automobiles in Germany were pretty interesting in those days. First of all, Mercedes were not only inexpensive because of the rate of exchange, but they also were the vehicles used by the taxi drivers. Granted, the taxi models were stripped down versions with diesel engines, but it seemed incongruous to see a Mercedes, with its American aura of wealth, used to taxi folks around. And then there were the Messerschmitts. Right after the war, the Messerschmitt company, which was famous for its warplanes, had taken the fuselages that remained and cut them in back of the propeller and in back of the second in-line seat. The result was a small automobile with outrigger wheels that was accessed through the top by raising what had been the plane's canopy. Another tiny vehicle was the Italian Isetta, whose whole front, steering wheel and all, opened out for access. It had three wheels and looked much like some of our current crop of eco cars — and survived front end crashes about as well.

Our first daughter, Julie, was born while we were stationed at McKee Barracks in Crailsheim. Though we had a small clinic supported by two physicians there, obstetrics was handled in the Army General Hospital in Bad Cannstadt on the outskirts of Stuttgart, a two-hour drive away over a winding two-lane blacktop Highway 14. The trick was to time your drive so that you arrived at Bad Cannstadt in time for the delivery. Helicopter Medevacs were reserved for serious emergencies, so husbands typically drove their wives to the hospital, which was much preferred to a two-hour ride in an Army field ambulance. If the timing was wrong, the fallback was to stop at the German hospital in Schwäbisch Hall, about halfway to Stuttgart. In those days, obstetrics in Germany was considerably behind the state of the art in the American practice, and the fallback was not a desirable alternative from the pregnant spouse's point of view. That made for some tense moments as the baby's due date approached. In our case, we managed it barely since my wife's water broke as we got out of the car in the Bad Cannstadt Army Hospital parking lot! A long twelve hours later, spent counting the bricks in the wall that faced the window of my wife's lying-in room, we became the proud parents of a lovely baby girl.

Prior to the Berlin Wall going up, the Eisenhower administration had been withdrawing troops from Europe, and curtailed tours had been common. After the Wall went up, there was a surge of reinforcements back to Europe, so I thought that I would have no trouble extending my tour and my battalion-level experience. I applied for an extension, only to get orders curtailing my tour because I had been selected for the next level of Army officer schooling. In mid-July 1962, we left West Germany with a six-week-old daughter, a practically new Mercedes to be shipped home at government expense, great professional experience, a lot of very good memories—and the mandatory cuckoo clock!

The flight back was a precursor of the flying challenges of the future. Jet service had been initiated between Europe and the United States, but we ended up once more on a four-engine Constellation charter. The amenities did not include the ability to heat baby bottles, so my wife sat on the bottle to warm it up prior to each feeding. By the time we reached the United States, we had been on both the planes that this particular charter airline company owned, changing to the second plane in Nova Scotia after a delay on the ground because of mechanical problems. That delay resulted in the plane being diverted from McGuire Air Force Base in New Jersey, where our parents were to meet us, to LaGuardia Airport in New York City. Since the authorities at LaGuardia were not used to Army charters landing there, we sat on the runway for a couple of hours, waiting for customs, with our six-week-old becoming increasingly unhappy and hungry. We finally got to the terminal, but our parents were at McGuire Air Force Base. So, we phoned McGuire and got a message through to them. Then, rather than waiting for them to drive back up to the New York City area, we took a cab to the Brooklyn Army Terminal, where our Mercedes had arrived. We then drove home to White Plains, arriving before our parents. The potential problems with air travel are both endless and timeless!

It would be eight years before we returned to West Germany.

11

THE BAD YEARS

Those eight years in the U.S. were taken up with a mid-level Army school, graduate school in preparation for teaching at the Military Academy at West Point, an interrupted four-year tour on the faculty of the Military Academy, promotion to major, a combat tour in Vietnam, and, finally, selection for the Army Command and General Staff College. As graduation from the Command and General Staff College approached, we faced a quandary. It appeared unlikely that we would spend more than a year in any assignment before I would be reassigned to Vietnam. The question was where would we rather spend that year? The opportunity to be assigned to the staff in the headquarters of USAREUR and Seventh Army (the two headquarters had been combined in Heidelberg during our years away) provided the answer. We knew something about living in West Germany, I knew something about USAREUR, and so the environment sounded just right from both a professional and a family perspective. We would enjoy it for as long as the Army saw fit to keep us there.

We transferred to Heidelberg, West Germany, in the summer of 1970, fully expecting that we would have a short tour of between twelve and eighteen months, and so we were determined to make the most of what we would be given before I was reassigned to Vietnam. We moved into a three-bedroom apartment in the housing area across the street from the USAREUR headquarters, which made it easy for me to walk to work and even come home for lunch on occasion. Trolley and bus transportation to downtown Heidelberg were available only two blocks from our apartment, and the elementary school was in walking distance for our oldest daughter.

I had no inkling of how conditions had changed in USAREUR during the eight years that separated our first tour from this second tour in West Germany. My initial assignment to the Policy and Statistics Branch of the Military Personnel Division in the Office of the Deputy Chief of Staff for Personnel quickly gave me a picture of how badly overall conditions in USAREUR had deteriorated.

The Military Personnel Division handled officer assignments and personnel policy issues, while the Policy and Statistics Branch focused on enlisted personnel support policies and balancing the gross allocations of enlisted personnel to USAREUR's major subordinate commands. From my new position, I quickly came to see how degraded USAREUR had become in the eight years that I had been away because of the drain of Vietnam.

Officers and noncommissioned officers were in short supply, as were critical enlisted skills. Maintenance funds for equipment and for facilities had been cut to fund the war in Vietnam. The result was equipment that didn't run and buildings that were practically uninhabitable due to boarded up broken windows and inoperable plumbing. Many "sanitary blocks" had only one of the six showerheads working. As a reflection of the times and the problems in the general population back in the States, drug usage was up, and racial tensions were running high. The Army policy of assigning junior enlisted men to USAREUR for the few months remaining in their terms of service after tours in Vietnam also gifted us with lots of bad attitudes. Finally, the lack of experienced leadership caused by the officer and noncommissioned officer shortages provided a vacuum in which those attitudes could take root and be acted out.

Hugh Bartley, my squadron commander in Vietnam, and later both a brigade commander and assistant division commander in Germany, characterized the situation as, the "perfect storm," to use one of today's favorite expressions, created by the convergence of racial tensions, the Volunteer Army program (known as VOLAR to one and all), leadership deficiencies, and administrative confusion. The racial tensions that were rife in the United States were kept alive in USAREUR by an underground that circulated the views of Malcolm X in the *Black Panther Solidarity News*, which featured pictures of black members of the military who were described as "black soldier . . . revolutionaries [ready] to overthrow the ruling class."

The VOLAR program was an attempt to make life more attractive for the junior enlisted men as the draft was phased out. It featured such new "reforms" as a five-day work week instead of the traditional five-and-a-half-day work week, elimination of reveille formation, limitation of other troop formations, elimination of the need for a "pass" to leave post for junior enlisted personnel, elimination of mileage restrictions that had limited the maximum distance from the unit that a soldier could travel when off duty, and elimination of bed check except for men serving punishment. Other relaxations of policies were also recommended, but "GI newspapers" insisted on keeping the pot boiling amongst both black and white soldiers alike by questioning the "real" motivation for these reforms. The failure of some units to adhere to the VOLAR guidance just added fuel to the fire.

Mixed into this already critical mass for unrest was the leadership deficiency already noted, which was aggravated by the strength imbalance between junior enlisted soldiers and officer and noncommissioned officer strength. The Army had decided to assign junior enlisted men departing Vietnam with as little as four months remaining on their commitments to USAREUR. The intent was to appear to be maintaining the strength of USAREUR while holding down the numbers needed after the about-to-be-eliminated draft took place.. Aside from the decreased interest in performance typical for a short-term combat veteran in the last months of service and the turmoil caused by that kind of turnover, these soldiers were frequently on the road and seemed to require an inordinate amount of travel to centralized facilities to take care of health issues, pay issues, and other personal end-of-tour problems. Solving these sometimes very real problems was made harder by administrative confusion in the system and the same lack of critical skills that was affecting all of USAREUR.

While this infusion of junior enlisted men with four months remaining in their enlistment might bring units to as much as 14% over the authorized strength on paper, the *Army Times* noted that many of these same units were up to 55% short of senior noncommissioned officers and had lieutenants commanding all company-size units (normally, these were captain commands). The situation caused one general officer to characterize USAREUR as being a combination of inexperience, incompetence, and cowards. Overly dramatic as that quotation might be, as the word got around, officers assignments branch at USAREUR headquarters started getting letters from incoming officers such as this one written by a major:

> I would prefer an assignment that will permit me to be at home at night most of the time [and] I would hope not to get into an impossible troop assignment consisting of personnel, morale, and disciplinary problems that would wreck my career. I would fight to avoid an assignment with those ramifications.

Finally, the Army chose this moment to introduce a new centralized pay system, which was accompanied by all the bugs that any large, new, standardized system always encounters. Very real pay problems were added to the grievances, real or imagined, that the short-term junior enlisted combat veterans had. Unfortunately, the problems overlapped. Not only did the new centralized pay system require frequent trips to the local finance office to fix mistakes, but the local finance office might well be manned by junior enlisted pay specialists without sufficient supervision who also had a short timer's attitude.

General Bartley, who became the USAREUR Comptroller after his tour as an assistant division commander, was out visiting finance offices one day when he found a long line queued up outside the shuttered service window of a finance office. It was well past the allotted period for the noon meal, so General Bartley went around to the back and knocked on the door. When it was opened, he found two specialists and their wives playing bridge while the troops waited in line for service. General Bartley got them back to work with some well-chosen words, but the two specialists then complained to the Inspector General that a general officer had embarrassed them in front of their wives. That complaint went nowhere, but it is illustrative of the attitude and the times.

As noted previously, the VOLAR effort was meant to improve service attractiveness for junior enlisted personnel. Aside from initiating the kinds of reforms that led to less structure at the very time when it was most needed, it also promised much more than it could quickly deliver. Beer and liquor allowed in barracks and the five-day workweek could be easily implemented, if at some sacrifice to unit effectiveness and good order and discipline, but the money and capability to implement many other initiatives such as "adventure training" was simply not immediately available. New requirements for better furniture (like a desk and single-decked 36-inch beds for each man) and minimum space (90 square feet per man) ran up against the constraints of funding and the old German barracks that we were using, which lacked the space to accommodate those new requirements. This was also the case with the promised additional amenities. There was no way to implement the proposals for coffee houses, rap shacks, soda fountains, and the like on the pre-World War II German *kasernes* that USAREUR units occupied. Unfortunately, the steady stream of advertising and press releases that accompanied VOLAR had raised the expectations of junior enlisted personnel—and supplied continued fodder for the always critical GI newspapers, such as the *Overseas Weekly*.

Predictably, indiscipline was rife. There were incidents of black soldiers taking over some of the small posts for short periods of time in an effort either to protest the admittedly terrible living conditions and the disparity between what had been advertised and what was reality or to express their attitudes on racial issues. So common had demonstrations become that General Polk, the Commander-in-Chief of USAREUR, saw fit to issue a command-wide letter on "Demonstrations and Public Gatherings by USAREUR Personnel." His guidance was to "prohibit gatherings whose objectives are incompatible with the command's mission" while being liberal in granting permission "for troops to gather on-post for legitimate purposes." The letter concluded by encouraging commanders to "be guided by a spirit of fairness in allowing maximum freedom of expression consistent with that responsibility." That guidance left a lot to the discretion of the overworked and understaffed lieutenant colonel commander on an isolated one- or two-battalion post.

Even the very personnel assignment system was vulnerable to disruption in this environment. One day I received a computer printout indicating that one of our divisions was over in the assignment of a critical skill that was also a critical shortage overall in the Army. After getting nowhere with the burgeoning data systems people in the headquarters, I called down to the division involved and was told that the skill in question was in fact still critically short in that unit. When I explained what I had encountered, the Personnel Warrant Officer with whom I was speaking said he would look into it. I got a phone call back a day or so later telling me that some young enlisted specialist with an attitude had simply been inputting the shortage skill for every new junior enlisted accession to the division, regardless of the actual skill of the man assigned.

The disaffection of the junior enlisted soldiers manifested itself most dramatically on Range 82 at Grafenwoehr, where tank crews are faced with overcoming simulated combat situations in which targets unexpectedly confront the crews at varying ranges. There were instances of tank crews intentionally missing targets, fumbling maneuvers, and otherwise deliberately failing to qualify in sullen resentment against an Army they detested. You hear some talk today about not ever returning to a draft because of that kind of memory. Folks assert that you would not have the esprit that you have in the all-volunteer Army, but that is simply wrong and another example of "tradition is what we did last year."

The draftee Army, properly led and sprinkled with folks who wanted to enlist, was a perfectly effective fighting force with which we successfully fought a World War, the Korean War, and the Vietnam War until late in the game. It gave us more college-educated soldiers, and it provided a melting pot in which all classes of society and all races learned to live and work as a team with each other. That was an important ingredient that helped to homogenize American society in a good way, but more importantly, it gave a sense of service to country to many of our young people that simply does not exist in America today.

Unfortunately, the VOLAR effort, whose focus was easing the transition from the draft to an all-volunteer Army, also relaxed or eliminated some of the traditional aspects of the Army's policies and discipline in an attempt to make the environment in which the volunteer junior enlisted soldiers would live more attractive. That caused resentment among the noncommissioned officers because it appeared to strike directly at their authority, and they stepped back from their responsibilities for a time. Interestingly, at the same time that we were relaxing the institutional policies and restrictions for junior enlisted men to make life in the barracks more attractive for them, we were getting survey data that showed most of the blue-collar enlistees were enlisting because they wanted a more structured environment than what was then available to them in the civilian culture of the early 1970s. Rather than shoring up the values that they sought, the Army appeared to be condoning sloppiness, thievery, violence, and "getting over" by the very reforms that were intended to make junior-enlisted life more attractive.

Colonel Richard J. Eaton, a brigade commander in the 3rd Infantry Division, may have captured the final irony in his required "Quarterly Improving Service Attractiveness Report." He noted that the soldiers in his brigade seem to "concern themselves intensely with shortages in tools and other resources directly related to their jobs, [while] they seem relatively apathetic about the many VOLAR-promised comfort and convenience items."

The situation in USAREUR was exacerbated by the very settings that had contributed to a sense of community and tightly knit units during our previous tour in Germany eight years before. The dispersion of the command in some 200 installations, some of them containing only one battalion and none of them containing more than four or five battalions, made for individual installation environments that depended very much on the personality, energy, and professionalism of the respective command structures. Given the shortages of personnel in leadership positions, it was no wonder that there were some weak spots where discipline was lax, facilities were allowed to deteriorate beyond the acceptable, and insufficient attention was paid to race relations. Many of these installations had only a small Military Police detachment consisting of several junior enlisted men commanded by a sergeant, so combating drug abuse was largely in the hands of this same over-stressed chain of command.

Into this chaos came the first Army Equal Opportunity survey team to visit USAREUR and document problems relating to racial tensions. The team found what we all knew: racial tensions were high, troop living conditions were poor, indiscipline was rife, and the whole was exacerbated by drug abuse. Not a pretty picture! The head of the survey team, Colonel Jim White, my old tent mate from my 1st Infantry Division days in Vietnam, had the unpleasant responsibility of reporting the team's findings to the Commander in Chief of USAREUR at the conclusion of the team's visit. General Polk, who had been such an effective division commander during my 4th Armored Division days, could not believe that the conditions that were outlined in the out-briefing were as bad as reported. He rejected the seriousness of the claims and dismissed Colonel White rather abruptly. Facts, however, were facts, and it was very apparent that action was needed to resolve the very real problems related to racial tensions that were manifesting themselves throughout the command. That chore fell to General Polk's successor, General Michael S. Davison.

As USAREUR worked against odds to counter the unacceptable results of drug abuse and racial tensions—both a reflection of the societal turmoil in the United States from which our young soldiers were emerging to join the Army—the television media did its part to further exacerbate the problem. One crusading television reporter cum-personality, then just beginning his career, journeyed to Berlin to report on the drug problem there. He found a private who was admittedly using drugs who assured him that all the officers in Berlin were also doing drugs. Despite the fact that it was a patently false statement, or that it was a given that most drug users were expert manipulators, that was the picture that he presented to his television viewers back in the United States, where his interview with the drug-using private was widely seen.

Possibly more egregious in terms of its impact was the work of a TV celebrity reporter from a prestigious network show known for its "special" reports. He came to do such a special report on race relations in USAREUR for his show. At his request, the Army had somewhat naively given him permission to interview some soldiers without any official escort present so that he could find out how they "really" felt about racial tensions. Two groups of soldiers were made available, one all white and one all black. Some of this celebrity reporter's assistants then proceeded to work up the emotions of the white soldiers so that they showed a high degree of hostility and aggressiveness in his opening shots, thus portraying the "white backlash" that he believed was feeding the problem. Neither of these TV personalities was interested in reporting the very real efforts being made to resolve the very real problems of drug abuse and racial tensions. In the end, those efforts did successfully resolve the problems of a very troubled period.

As if General Davison did not have enough on his menu, he also faced a rate of exchange problem that saw the value of the dollar decreasing against the German deutsche mark shortly after he arrived. Though USAREUR had no control over rates of exchange, and, of course, had nothing to do with global money markets, the fluctuating rate of exchange created huge problems financially for a command that was funded in U.S. dollars—not to mention for the personal budgets of the individual members of the command. Every *pfennig* change in the rate of exchange between the deutsche mark and the dollar caused thousands of dollars in decreased financial resources for the USAREUR budget.

The man responsible for overseeing that budget and answering to General Davison for the decreased financial resources was my ex-commander from the cavalry squadron with which I had served in Vietnam. Hugh Bartley, by now a brigadier general, was the Comptroller for USAREUR. He was at the mercy of the international money markets, but had to answer to his commander for circumstances over which he had no control. General Bartley worked out his frustrations one day by showing up unannounced at the Headquarters USAREUR administrative motor pool and performing a very thorough inspection of the vehicles and maintenance area in the kind of detail that is the specialty of an experienced armor commander. He left a thoroughly befuddled motor sergeant who could not figure out who had inspected him or why he had been so thoroughly critiqued. General Bartley remarked that at least in that motor pool, he knew what he was doing!

Despite the problems that faced USAREUR, living in the Heidelberg community enabled us to participate in any number of German-American activities because of the very active German-American clubs and friendship societies. The military personnel assigned to the headquarters were heavily engaged in these community activities, and the USAREUR Headquarters policy was to encourage such activities. It was to everybody's advantage to maintain a close relationship between the military community and the German makers and shakers of opinion in the Heidelberg community. As a result, we had more opportunities to get to know German families and made friendships that have lasted to this day.

One of the most popular activities that the headquarters sponsored once or twice a year was an American *Volksfest*. These were patterned after the German *Volksfests*, which were a standby of every small German town—occasions to showcase the particular town and its wine or produce, much like our county fairs. The American *Volksfest* consisted of the best features of both America and Germany: county fair-style booths manned by volunteers selling American specialties and huge tents in which the attendees could listen and dance to "oompah" bands and consume beer and sausage or hamburgers and ice cream. The ice cream booth was a huge attraction for the German folks, who flocked to these American *Volksfests* because our ice cream in that era was much richer and creamier than the German product. The Germans would buy huge quantities of the ice cream and store it in insulated containers that they had brought with them.

The benches inside the tents were a place to mingle, with German and American families interspersed next to each other trading stories and dancing polkas with each other, regardless of nationality. Many, including our family, made life-long friends as a result of sitting next to a German family with whom you just hit it off. It was a wonderful way to raise money for otherwise unfunded support activities such as scouting and to get to know our German hosts and become known to them in a relaxed and informal atmosphere.

As we marked our one-year anniversary in USAREUR, it became apparent that a combination of factors was going to enable us to stay for longer than the twelve to eighteen months that we had expected. The drawdown of our forces in Vietnam had begun and there simply was not the requirement for Armor majors that there had been just a year before. By then, the long drawn-out peace negotiations had started in Paris, and that decreased requirements for the foreseeable future even more. In addition, as the needs of Vietnam lessened, the Army became very sensitive to the havoc that the war effort had created in West Germany. Increased funding started to trickle in, and an effort was made to fill the critical slots and to stabilize the officer and noncommissioned officer tours at close to the traditional three years. It now appeared that we would actually serve a full three-year tour in USAREUR despite what we had expected when we embarked on the tour.

After about a year and a half in the personnel business, I was selected to become one of the three Assistant Secretaries to the General Staff. Our job was to review all the staff papers that came to the USAREUR Command Group for the approval and signature of the Commander in Chief or his Major-General Chief of Staff. The staff papers recommended decisions, and the respective signatures approved the decision. We looked for unanswered questions or hidden problems in these papers, ensured that the papers were clearly written so that they could be easily absorbed by the decision makers, and arranged for the responsible staffs to brief the papers to provide additional background if needed. In addition, we helped to ensure that the Command Group functioned smoothly, writing short speeches for the members of the Command Group as needed or coordinating Command Group activities. It was a wonderful position from which to view the overall operation of USAREUR and to observe how the Command Group's three senior generals, the Chief of Staff, the Deputy Commander in Chief, and the Commander in Chief, operated.

Some five months later, my exposure in that job gave me the opportunity to apply for the position of Senior Aide to the Lieutenant-General Deputy Commander in Chief when that position became vacant due to normal rotation. I was fortunate enough to be selected for the position and embarked on a year of the best training for command that I ever received in the Army.

12

THE RECOVERY

Though better personnel, financial, and logistical support was starting to flow into USAREUR, the command was a long way from achieving the combat readiness that was the goal and that had existed prior to the onset of the Vietnam conflict. Among the issues that were in crisis in USAREUR when General Michael S. Davison assumed the position of Commander in Chief (CINC) was the state of training throughout the command. Training simply was not being accomplished or, if attempted, was being done poorly. Training schedules were dutifully drawn up, but the training rarely took place as scheduled, and if it took place at all, it was rarely effective. There were, of course, exceptions that resulted from a few very professional field grade officers doing what they were supposed to do against the odds presented by the current environment.

Colonel Hugh Bartley wrote a memo to his 2nd Brigade, 3rd Armored Division, when he was the brigade commander that caught the essence of what was needed:

> The brigade commander's primary role, as I see it, is one of a manager; it is that of so arranging the administrative matters related to training so as to optimize the battalion commander's opportunities to train his battalion. I would say, as a rough rule of thumb, that the more I get involved in how well you are

training your battalion, the less well I think you are doing it and the more attention you should accordingly pay to it.

Unfortunately, all too few brigade commanders took this view initially, and all too few battalion commanders understood initially the full extent of the implied responsibility.

A year later, when Colonel Bartley had been promoted to brigadier general and had been reassigned as the Assistant Division Commander of the 3rd Infantry Division, he summed up the state of training very well in a memo he wrote to the commanding general of the division after a visit to the major training area at Hohenfels to observe division training. After remarking on the amount of unnecessary gear that armored-vehicle crews take to the field (so much that critical items like overshoes, spare socks, and crew helmets were overlooked) and the lack of radio discipline (too much chatter on command nets), he summed it all up by saying, "We are, in a way, like children who have difficulty mastering a basic skill and must be run back through the creeping and crawling stages to mature properly!"

The reasons for this state of affairs had to do, once more, with the strain that the Vietnam effort had put on every aspect of USAREUR. Officers and noncommissioned officers and critical enlisted skills had been in short supply, and the length of the tour for those in theater had been uncertain, depending on the needs of Vietnam and the training base in the United States. In addition, there were the distractions of the indiscipline, the racial tensions, and the generally poor condition of the facilities theater wide.

General Davison believed that training was all-encompassing and impacted far more than weapons qualification or tactical maneuver proficiency. Based on this belief, he assigned his new Deputy Commander in Chief (DCINC) the responsibility for improving training throughout the command. The position of DCINC had a wide-ranging menu of possible areas of focus. Each

Commander in Chief would choose the areas that he wanted emphasized from that menu, and General Davison chose training in its broadest sense.

He could not have picked a better man for the job than Lieutenant General Arthur S. Collins, known far and wide as "Ace" because of the appearance of his scrawled initials indicating that he had seen or approved this or that official paper. General Collins, a banty Boston Irishman and a product of Boston Latin School, graduated from the U.S. Military Academy in 1938 at the age of twenty-two and rose to the rank of colonel and command of an infantry regiment in the Pacific Theater by the age of twenty-seven during World War II. He was the archetypical teacher and trainer, having served stints on the faculties of West Point and the Army War College and been the infantry advisor to the South Korean Army. He had assumed command of the 4th Infantry Division at Fort Lewis, Washington, and had trained it for deployment before taking it to Vietnam. After serving as an Assistant Chief of Staff for Force Development on the Army staff at the Pentagon, he had returned to Vietnam as the commander of the I Field Force (the equivalent of a corps command). He assumed the position of DCINC after that assignment, arriving in 1971. General Collins had a strong aversion to showy demonstrations of the kind subordinates dearly love to put on for general officers. That aversion, along with a grassroots approach and an extraordinary grasp of training essentials, combined to provide the perfect instrument for achieving General Davison's goal of improving overall combat readiness in USAREUR.

When I joined General Collins's team in May 1972 as his Senior Aide, the routine was already well established. We visited units in USAREUR at one or another of the almost 200 installations four days a week and caught up on administration and the DCINC's other responsibilities on the fifth day. The Junior Aide, Captain Ron Joe, or I accompanied the General on every trip and wrote a trip report of the General's observations immediately on our return. That report went to the CINC and the senior commanders involved, possibly augmented by a phone call from General Collins to the general officer in whose area we had been visiting—and frequently that officer would initiate the call to find out more quickly what had been observed.

These reports focused on the two key principles that General Collins believed were the basis for good training: training is all encompassing and should be related to everything the unit does or can have happen to it, and it is the responsibility of the general officers and full colonels to create an atmosphere in which effective training can take place. Those were the areas he looked at during our visits, and those were the areas that were reported on in the trip reports. The performance of the company and battalion commanders at the units we visited were the measure of the first principle, and what we learned from soldiers and officers at the units we visited was the measure of the second principle.

General Collins believed strongly that his visits needed to be unannounced because of the tendency to put on a show if subordinates knew that a general was coming and because of the time wasted by those who believed they needed to also be in attendance. He wanted to see things as they were every day, understanding that there would be some activities that were not perfect, and he did not want the chain of command standing around waiting for him when they should be supervising their soldiers.

Along with the immediate preparation of the trip report when we returned to headquarters, the other thing that Captain Joe and I could count on was being asked if we had paid for any drink or meal that might have been consumed by the general. It mattered not how small the amount involved had been, the answer had better be that we had reimbursed the host on the spot for any drink or food that had been consumed. That might not be a bad guideline for all leaders in this day and age, but it was an ironclad rule within

General Collins's team. In point of fact, we rarely took time for the noon meal because the General was well aware of the disruption that it could cause in a mess hall, but if we did, we had better have paid up before we left.

Since our visits were always unannounced—and therefore caused some level of anxiety for commanders from company to brigade throughout USAREUR—there was a great deal of command-wide interest in trying to determine where we were going to visit next. A simple procedure prevented that from ever actually happening, at least to the best of my knowledge. The General would tell us where we were going the night before, on the way to the Heidelberg Army Airfield, or once we were aboard the helicopter supplied by the flight detachment supporting the USAREUR Headquarters Command Group. Lest somebody figure out that they could tap into our flight plan and thus learn our destination, we exploited flight planning rules to the maximum by not declaring our destination until we were on short final for landing, typically about three minutes out. The result was that every visit was a total surprise—which led to some fascinating results aside from discovering whether there was effective, all-encompassing training or whether the environment existed in which effective training could even take place. The one thing that everybody did come to know was that if either of those areas were found to be lacking, they could be assured of a second unannounced visit within a week to ten days. That was the General's way of following up to see if the unit visited had learned from his first visit.

Of course, landing unannounced at a small airfield left us on our own for ground transportation to the nearby *kaserne*. General Collins frequently solved that problem by simply hailing a vehicle and driver that happened to be at the airfield, which gave him the opportunity to chat with the driver on the drive to the *kaserne*. The soldier was normally charmed to have a three-star riding in the cab with him, and by the time that we reached the *kaserne*, General

Collins knew how the driver felt about the food and conditions in the barracks, as well as when he had last fired his weapon and how well he maintained his vehicle.

For instance, we landed at Bamberg one day and found an aviation fuel tanker and its driver near the runway. General Collins asked if the driver would give us a ride into the post—and not many drivers were going to say "no" to a three-star. After making some small talk, the general asked the driver what kind of problems he had. The driver responded that he couldn't get his brakes fixed even though he had reported the problem. While that indicated that we should go look at the motor pool and talk to the driver's platoon leader and maintenance sergeant, the bigger issue was that a fuel tanker was not supposed to move if it didn't have brakes for very obvious safety reasons. This was a typical example of the leads we got from our impromptu transportation arrangements. Any soldier responses to these kinds of questions that indicated problems prompted more digging in the respective areas.

Having arrived on post in a fuel tanker, a 2-1/2 ton truck, an ambulance, or some other vehicle that happened to be available at the airfield, there was no signal to anybody that the DCINC was loose within the *kaserne*. It always amazed me how long it took for the word to get to the senior commander on post that he was being inspected by a three-star general. In too many instances, the length of time was proportional to the problems we would find. By the time the responsible lieutenant colonel or colonel found us in problem units, we would have spent an hour or two checking on training and the condition of the facilities where that training was supposed to be taking place. General Collins would find a company commander or a platoon leader and ask to see his training schedule. He would then select a training event from among those scheduled as being conducted at that moment and ask to be taken to it. Classroom training always drew the General's eye, and he would frequently select such training for his first stop.

Since many training classrooms were in the barracks, we would get to see their condition on our way. If a squad room or hall looked to be in poor condition, we would detour into it. That might lead to checking other floors to see if they were all in that condition. Eventually, we would get to the classroom where we, at least initially in our travels, would find an empty room or, at best, a room with a few soldiers shooting the bull. We would then seek out the next higher commander of our requisitioned escort, a company or battalion commander most probably, and the general would inquire as to why the training schedule was not being followed and why that commander was unaware that it was not taking place. That discussion would probably be followed by a request to go to some other problem area that General Collins had identified with the driver of the vehicle that had given us a ride in from the airfield, like the motor pool to which that fuel tanker belonged in Bamberg.

While the 1st Armored Division units and the one squadron of the 2nd Armored Cavalry stationed at Bamberg were no better or worse than similar units at other locations, we seemed to end up or make an interim stop at Bamberg fairly frequently. On one memorable occasion early on in my stint as General Collins's aide, we had a function to attend in Nuremberg in the early evening in civilian clothes, after which we were going to Bamberg for a rare scheduled visit. After the function, we drove to Bamberg in an Army sedan. As we drove through the main gate of Warner Barracks en route to the Visiting Officers Quarters, the General suddenly decided to detour to the enlisted men's club.

There had been reports of racial tensions centered on that club, and the reports had stated that black soldiers had decided that it should be a black-only club, excluding their white peers. General Collins wanted to see for himself what the conditions were and judge the ambiance. I had a concern about the General's safety, but he was having none of it. So, we pulled up outside the club at about 11 p.m., and off he went with me following close behind, both in civilian clothes. I am a little over 5' 8", and the General was a trifle shorter, so I lost him almost immediately after we entered the club and he started to circulate among the all-black patrons. As I tried to locate him ahead of me, I started to hear angry comments. Fortunately, about the time I caught up with him, the club manager had recognized him and was standing next to him. He chatted with a number of soldiers in the now completely calm atmosphere before we took ourselves off to our accommodations for the night. He had gained some insights into what the black soldiers were thinking, but I have never forgotten the scare when General Collins disappeared into that hostile crowd in front of me.

The following day we looked at the training that, this time, we had been invited to witness by the brigade commander. Skipping the offered lunch, as was the General's custom, we lifted off in a borrowed 1st Armored Division helicopter around noon to fly down to the Army Recreation Center at Berchtesgaden where there was a conference that General Collins was scheduled to participate in. On lifting off, the General asked the two very young warrant officers if they had flown to Berchtesgaden before because there was some tricky navigation involved as you wove your way along the valleys into the town, which was nestled among the mountains of the Alps. After being assured that they were up to the task, we carried on an intercom conversation about what we had seen and the upcoming schedule, all the while watching our progress through the closed passenger-door window.

A while later we started to take a bit more interest in our surroundings as we felt the helicopter bank into a left turn that led it into a valley. Though both the General and I had flown into Berchtesgaden before, we didn't remember such a turn and we didn't recognize any of the familiar landmarks. Then we felt the helicopter bank more sharply as it made a 180-degree turn to the right to avoid flying into the mountain face that marked the end of the valley. Poor map reading had led us down a blind valley.

The General followed our route on the ground as we headed back out of the valley. When the mouth of the valley came in sight, along with a small town, General Collins got on the intercom and told our lost pilots to put the ship down in the flat soccer field that was just coming up in front of us. There was a moment's silence from up front, but before either warrant officer could object, General Collins commanded, "Put it down right there, now!" And down we went.

We jumped out once on the ground, and the General waved the helicopter off. We walked into town, found a pleasant coffee shop, and enjoyed some good German coffee and pastry while I called a thoroughly puzzled post commander at Berchtesgaden, explained where we were, and asked for transportation to pick us up. A sedan carrying the post commander arrived after a bit, and we went on with the scheduled events. Minor though this incident may seem, it is indicative of the man (calm, incisive, and unconcerned with the trappings of his rank) and the state of training in USAREUR at that moment. I never followed up on the two pilots, other than to report the incident to the parent commander, but I suspect they had a goodly amount of explaining to do as to why their mission was aborted. From General Collins's point of view, it was a training opportunity, and the teaching point could not have been more dramatically made.

On those rare occasions that General Collins thought it important to arrive at a visit site very early in the morning, we would make use of the USAREUER Command Train that was available to us. There were two of these trains, each consisting of a parlor/dining car with a galley and a sleeping car with a master suite and a number of smaller sleeping compartments. One train was assigned to the CINC and the other, which had been the Seventh Army commander's train before the headquarters consolidation, to the DCINC. They were left over from the occupation days and were an admitted luxury, but they were also a great convenience, and completely paid for by the West German government. Arrangements would be made with the *Bundsebahn*, the German national railroad system, to hook the cars on to the appropriate trains to get us to our destination on time. We would board in the early evening at the siding in Heidelberg, where the trains were maintained, and after a comfortable night, arrive in the early morning hours at the rail siding of the town nearest to the *kaserne* that we were interested in visiting.

We used this Command Train, for instance, when General Collins wanted to start a visit to Christensen Barracks at Bindlach, a short distance north of Bayreuth, early in the morning. Christensen Barracks was home to a squadron of the 2nd Armored Cavalry Regiment and was an isolated post for which the squadron commander, a lieutenant colonel, was also the post commander. Such isolated posts could either function very well or very poorly depending entirely on the lieutenant colonel. Either way, they tended to get less attention from their chains of command than the more accessible posts and units and were therefore a magnet for the DCINC'S attentions. After making the necessary arrangements with the *Bundesbahn*, we boarded the train in Heidelberg in the early evening and found ourselves on a siding next to the railroad station in Bindlach in the early hours of the following morning.

We disembarked and found a taxi at the station to take us to Christensen Barracks, where we were dropped off at the front gate. We walked through the front gate, exchanging salutes with the military police in the gatehouse and found the unit mess hall. Breakfast was being served so we mingled with the diners, the General chatting easily with the soldiers while he checked the serving line, the food, the general cleanliness, and the overall environment of the dining facility. We then went looking for some training. We must have walked around the post for almost two hours, and checked at least two training sites, before the commander found out that the DCINC was there and joined up with us. We continued on, with the commander in tow, checking out additional training and eventually ending up in the unit motor pool. General Collins then debriefed the commander about the good and not-so-good things that he had encountered, and we left around noon on a helicopter that had flown up from Heidelberg at our request. The length of time it had taken for the commander to be notified of our presence had been a precursor to what we found, and we were back in about ten days to see if the lessons had been learned. Apparently they had been.

If weather interfered with our flying, the fallback was a short drive by sedan to Mannheim, some thirty kilometers to the northwest of Heidelberg. There were a number of installations located around the outskirts of that city that we could pick from, but Turley Barracks, a small post close to where General Patton's sedan had been hit by a truck in the accident that proved fatal to the general shortly after the end of World War II, was the recipient of many of our visits. It was home to some general support companies (transportation, maintenance, or ordnance organizations assigned to support the entire theater) whose supervisory chain of command was typically at a good distance from the individual support companies. The opportunity for problems with these types of separate companies whose next high headquarters was nowhere near them and who were commanded by young captains was great.

General Collins's fascination with Turley Barracks started when we stopped there one rainy day for a routine unannounced visit. As usual, we found a junior officer and asked for his training schedule. The training that the General indicated he wanted to see was supposed to be taking place on the top floor of one of the old-style German barracks of which the post consisted, so off we went. We entered the stairwell at one end of the barracks where the training was supposed to be taking place and started to climb to the fourth floor. When we reached the second floor, it became apparent that the stairwell above us was filled with trash and that nobody had been above the second floor in this end stairwell for some time. Apparently the local solution to emptying trashcans was to simply throw their contents into the stairwell instead of taking them out to the dumpster that stood beside the barracks. How long that practice had been going on was hard to say, but the stairwell was filled from the second floor up. Needless to say, General Collins was not thrilled by his discovery of the housekeeping practices or the fact that despite the training schedule, nobody had been above the second floor landing in a very long time. In addition, there was the fact that the officers seemed unaware of either problem. Thereafter, Turley Barracks became a regular rainy day destination—though we never encountered again any of the original leaders that we had met on that first visit. Despite a dramatic turnover of officers at Turley Barracks, it must have been almost a year of repeat visits before it started to pass muster.

Somewhere during this period, the Army introduced "Adventure Training" into the equation as part of the Volunteer Army effort. The idea was that small units should go off on some typical civilian adventure like mountain climbing or skiing or rafting to give the soldiers a break from their training routine and build better esprit. That may have worked well in the business world for developing managers and teamwork, but it had doubtful results in the Army and was one more distraction that got in the way of the hard training that was required to rebuild an effective Army. Colonel Eaton, a brigade commander at Kitzingen in the 3rd Infantry Division, probably summed up the problem best when he noted in his "Quarterly Improving Service Attractiveness Report" that he "[did] not believe the exotic trip ('Down the Danube in Inner Tubes') is an essential part of this program." Instead, he hoped that "we can encourage imaginative company and platoon exercises which can be planned and carried out in two to four weeks. They should require no inordinately elaborate political and financial arrangements and should become fairly routine . . ."

A more humorous take on "Adventure Training" came from then-Colonel George Price, a brigadier general in the making and the brother of Leontyne Price, the opera singer. We had dropped into his brigade in the 3rd Infantry Division in Aschaffenburg and were about to depart after a good visit—Colonel Price was doing the things that General Collins was trying to promote, and the training that we had seen showed it—when the General asked him what he was doing about "Adventure Training." Colonel Price looked him in the eye and without a pause said, "General, it is enough of an adventure for my men to get themselves out of the motor pool during an alert."

Colonel Price would be one of the first generation of black general officers, and I had a rare insight into what these men had gone through to get to where they were a few months later in Garmisch at the annual USAREUR Equal Opportunity Conference. Both Captain Joe, the junior aide, and I had accompanied the DCINC to the conference, which ran for a full three days. The evenings were a time to mingle, and there were few official functions on the agenda during the evening hours so we aides were free to entertain ourselves.

Captain Joe was black, and through him I was invited to join a very special group for dinner that consisted of Captain Joe, another black captain who was aide to a black general officer, and the three black general officers who were present at the conference, Brigadier General Price among them. The stories that the three generals told during that very relaxed evening were amazing. Bear in mind that all three had joined the Army in the 1940s, some as enlisted men, and all in a segregated Army. They had survived segregation, war, and prejudice to achieve general officer rank, and they could laugh about some of the situations that they had faced. It was a very special evening for this white officer to have been included in. There is all too little credit given to the Army for its role in attempting to achieve not only total integration, but also total equal opportunity. What failures there have been in achieving that totality have not been the fault of either policy or a lack of good will on the part of most members of our Army.

Two events from my pre-commissioning days stand out to demonstrate just how far we had come by that winter of 1973. The first occurred when I was a cadet at The Citadel, the Military College of South Carolina, in 1953, prior to my entering the U.S. Military Academy at West Point. During the year that I was there, the ROTC program came due for its periodic Army Inspector General inspection that certifies that a program is meeting Army standards. There was a black captain on the inspection team, and the Citadel cadets steadfastly refused to salute him with no repercussions for this flagrant violation of Army regulations. To put that transgression in context, the Citadel's "fight flag" at football games in those days was the Confederate battle flag, and the Citadel cadets boasted that it was their predecessors who had fired the opening shots of the Civil War when they fired on the Union ship, *Star of the West*, which was sent to resupply Fort Sumter in the Charleston harbor. In fact, the *Star of the West* was the name of the Citadel's annual award for the outstanding cadet.

The second event occurred during summer training while I was a cadet at the Military Academy in 1957. We were on a class trip that took us to the various major Army training centers for the respective Army branches so that we would better understand what each did before we selected the branch in which we wanted to be commissioned. At Fort Benning, Georgia, we encountered an outstanding black Infantry officer. In conversation, we learned that he could not, of course, socialize with his fellow officers off post because he was not welcome in establishments that white officers would frequent. But then, my own roommate, of Italian descent who tanned deeply in the sun, had been stopped for being in a white-only line to the movies on suspicion of being black. Society and the Army had come a long way even by 1973.

As in any organization, however, there were always examples of arrogance that reminded you of what can happen if an institution is not vigilant. One minor example that got squashed occurred at Aschaffenburg with General Price's brigade commander successor. For some reason known only to this colonel, he had declared the helipad nearest to the *kaserne* to be off limits to all but full colonels (o6) and above, thus prohibiting any helicopter not carrying that kind of rank as passengers from landing there. Following our normal procedure, we landed there one day with only the three-minute warning available from filing our flight plan as we turned on short final to land. Apparently, the local airfield had called the brigade headquarters to alert the colonel that an unidentified helicopter without the qualifying rank aboard was violating his policy by landing on "his" helipad.

Before our rotor blades had stopped turning, the colonel, who apparently had nothing better to do, came on the run, obviously intent on correcting whoever had dared to violate his edict. Through the window I could see the disapproval and anger in his face as he huffed to our helicopter, and over the shoulder of General Collins, I watched the transformation in expression as the passenger door slid open and he was confronted with the nine stars visible on General Collins's field uniform—three on his hat and three on each shoulder of his field jacket. Such events broke up the usual seriousness of our visits.

We encountered a variety of interesting events in our travels, two of the more memorable of which had to do with our periodic visits to the other national armies located in West Germany. On one such visit to the British Army of the Rhine, which occupied the British sector in northern Germany, we were treated to very professional tank training being conducted by the storied British noncommissioned officers in a spotless indoor tank park. We were then taken to an adjacent paddock where a corporal was practicing spearing a ring with a lance from horseback at the gallop. This was a battalion from the Guards Regiment, and it had taken both its tanks and its horses on its rotation from England to the British Army of the Rhine—and was obviously intent on maintaining its proficiency in both types of mounted warfare. The hands-on training being conducted for both eras of weaponry was exactly the kind of training General Collins approved of.

The other memorable trip was to the *Bundeswehr* Tank Training Center in northern Germany. There we watched tank gunnery and tank field exercises conducted under the command of Lieutenant Colonel von Stauffenberg, the son of the Colonel Claus von Stauffenberg who led the failed attempt to kill Hitler in the closing days of World War II. It was very obvious that the *Bundeswehr* was taking care of the son of the famous father.

But what I remember most clearly about this trip occurred in the late afternoon after we had seen all the training events on our itinerary. The general was invited for coffee and pastries in the office of the training center commander. This brigadier general, and his two full colonel assistants, entertained General Collins in the casual environment of the commander's office, which was more like a Bavarian parlor in its furniture and ambiance than an official government office. The effect was enhanced by the pale north German sun streaming through the mullioned windows.

I was privileged to sit in the second row in back of the circle of the four veterans of World War II while they exchanged stories and talked about the training that we had witnessed. As the group became more relaxed, the three German officers, all veterans of Heinz Guderian's 1939 armor attack into Poland, started to kid each other about their wounds and what qualified each to be called a veteran. Like so many of the early *Bundeswehr* senior officers, these three all bore the scars of their experience—an arm that was not quite straight, a limp, a hand that did not quite work. One of the colonels remarked that the other colonel had missed too much of the fighting on the Polish front to claim to be a veteran of that combat because he had been left for dead on the field and only recovered after the fighting had ebbed. The other responded that unless you were wounded twenty-one times, as he had been, you could hardly count yourself a true veteran of the war.

And so it went, until it was time for us to depart. But what remains is the puzzle of the values of the regular German Army officer corps of World War II juxtaposed against the regime that they served. The care taken of von Stauffenberg, the son, and the conversation of these three veteran professionals somehow did not mesh with the horrors of the Nazi regime. Through all my years of service in Germany the dichotomy between Germans whom I came to know well, both civilian and military, and the Germans of the Nazi regime has remained a puzzle to me.

The puzzle was replicated when I came in contact with the efforts of the Baader-Meinhof [Red Army Faction] gang, a group of anarchists who wreaked havoc in West Germany during the 1970s. Their stock in trade was kidnapping influential members of the German banking or corporate world, some of whom they killed. They also made an occasional foray into bombing American military facilities. Campbell Barracks, the USAREUR Headquarters compound in Heidelberg, was a walled facility with manned gates on its four sides, but at that time, it was an open post into which anybody could drive without showing identification under normal circumstances. The Baader-Meinhof gang took advantage of this situation one late afternoon and drove a car loaded with explosives into the compound and parked it at the back of Campbell Barracks, outside the building that housed the post movie theater and some special signal facilities.

Captain Joe and I were closing up the DCINC's office after General Collins had left for his quarters, which were right behind the Command Building across a small, grassed area, when the car bomb went off. Both of us were Vietnam veterans, and there was no question in our minds as to what had taken place. The only question was the location of the explosion. We raced out the back door of the Command Building and into the DCINC's quarters. The quarters appeared empty, and we dashed into the dining room. The sight that we encountered there stopped us short. The table was set for two and the meals were partially eaten, but what caught our eye was the glass that was strewn everywhere. A line of windows high in the wall had stretched from one end of the room to the other overlooking the long side of the table. All that glass had been blown on to the long table, the floor, and the overturned chairs. We looked under the table, but there was no sign of the General or his wife.

Eventually, we found the back door open and the private gate through the wall into Campbell Barracks open. Following that trail, we found that General and Mrs. Collins had run to the sound of the explosion to see what they could do to help. Fortunately, the movie was still being shown when the bomb went off, and the theater was set far enough back in the low building that it was not disturbed. The occupants of the special signal center were not so fortunate. The outcome there was deadly.

I called my wife as quickly as I could to tell her I was all right, and by the time that I got home, one of the German couples with whom we had become friendly had called to express their horror at the memories that the column of smoke rising from the compound had brought back to them. The puzzle was that this couple and another with whom we had been friendly—both the husbands were lawyers and very much in tune with some of the more radical students at Heidelberg University, from which they had both graduated—had completely disappeared from the scene by the time we returned to Heidelberg some four years later. We could find no trace of them, nor anybody who knew where they might have gone, but the intervening years had seen the Baader-Meinhof gang hunted down and the radical student element pretty well isolated, their causes out of vogue. The puzzle, of course, was that these two couples could have been so friendly with us and yet so involved in an effort that was inimical to us.

After the attack on Campbell Barracks, the predictable bomb threats were phoned in to both the dependent schools and the Command Building. Some were pranks, but one never could be sure. The schools met the challenge of prank phoned-in bomb threats after the first few disruptions caused by evacuating the school buildings by assigning every class to a set of those old maid's quarters located on the fourth floor of each nearby family housing apartment building. That meant that if a bomb threat was received, the class simply moved to the fourth floor of its assigned apartment building and carried on sitting on the floor. The incidence of prank bomb threats dropped markedly.

The Command Building was a slightly different story. It was a two-story, smallish rectangular building set right on the street, to one side of and outside the walls of Campbell Barracks. There was a basement entrance under the nearest wall that could be entered through a locked, manned security gate during regular duty hours from Campbell Barracks, and Military Police manned the one front door 24-hours a day. The ground floor was largely glass in the back with an occasional set of French doors that opened on to the small garden that separated the headquarters building from the DCINC's quarters. There was no way to evacuate the building without spilling out onto Roemerstrasse, the four-lane major boulevard that connected with the center of Heidelberg. It was therefore decided that we would ignore all bomb threats.

The small size of the building, the restricted entry, and the dedicated Military Police detachment made it fairly easy to secure the building, but there was always a bit of suspense as we went about our business and the clock wound around to the hour that the bomb threat had specified for detonation. Car bombs were in their infancy at that time, and more sophisticated weapons had not yet come into play for the terrorists. It was not too many years later, however, that the CINC's sedan was the target of a rocket-propelled grenade. Fortunately, by that time the CINC had been supplied with an armored sedan.

As the DCINC's visits continued, we started to see improvement. More training took place in the field using the actual equipment that would be used if we went to war. Officers were more knowledgeable about the training being conducted in their units and more often than not had already checked the activity before we arrived on the scene. On occasion, the General would still drop down behind a machine gun in a tactical exercise and find that the gun clearance was obstructed by a rise in the ground a few feet in front of the barrel, to the chagrin of the sergeant or lieutenant in charge. Rather than this being a "gotcha" moment, it was a teaching moment. It was teaching leaders to see what they needed to see in order to create a trained, effective unit.

Not only did the DCINC teach them to look at the gun muzzle clearance as well as the fields of fire, but he taught them to check the seals on the external fire extinguishers as we walked by armored fighting vehicles in the motor pool and to notice the trailer-connecting pigtails that were sitting in accumulated water in the trailer beds because they were not hung from their brackets at the front end of those trailers. An additional indicator of improvement was that tank companies were qualifying sixteen out of seventeen tanks on Range 82 at Grafenwoehr, with the lone disqualifier repeating the course and frequently scoring among the top three or four on the second attempt. That was a return to the standards of ten years earlier.

We began to see more practical training that was better planned, more specificity in the training schedule as to what was supposed to be accomplished in the listed training, and more unannounced visits from all levels of the supervising chain of command. The aggregate of all those visits and all those trip reports had established a standardized basis for effective training across the theater, and the awareness that the DCINC might visit any unit on any given day added the motivation needed for senior leaders to provide the environment for this effective training. Along the way, the increased involvement of the chain of command in everyday training had also led to more awareness of soldier problems and facility problems. That in turn led to an increased capacity to deal with discipline, drug abuse, and racial tensions. Improved funding and stabilized tours for officers and senior noncommissioned officers as we drew down our presence in Vietnam multiplied the effect of these efforts.

Drew Middleton, the distinguished military analyst for the *New York Time* during that period, wrote in a July 1974 article entitled "Vietnam Behind It, U.S. Army in Europe Sets Efficient Pace," that General Collins had told General Davison that, "The yeast is in the bread, and it's working. We're on our way." Middleton defined the "yeast" as "the combination of innovation, drive, and sweaty effort" that Collins had introduced into the training. He credited Collins's "introduction of decentralized training [as] a major step in [USAREUR'S] recovery. Brigade and battalion officers decided what training was needed. Company commanders decided how the training was to be done." He quoted General Collins as saying, "Sure, some of them made mistakes. But they got to know their men and when they did, it was easier to handle problems like race and drugs and drink." Middleton concluded that USAREUR "was emerging from the post-Vietnam doldrums and was slowly developing into a skilled and professional force." He went on to say that "Non-American professional opinion" agreed.

The article was written just prior to General Collins's retirement in 1974. By then, USAREUR had solved many of the problems that had degraded its readiness in 1970 and 1971. The legacy of General Collins's work in the intervening years is codified in his book, *Common Sense Training: A Working Philosophy for Leaders*, which may still be the best primer available on effective training.

One night after dinner on the Command Train coming back from a trip to Berlin, I asked General Collins if the Army he was trying to build had ever really existed. I suspected then, and know now, that that Army he envisioned always existed around Ace Collins—and probably only around him. And that was all right because for those of us who had the privilege of working with him, that was the only Army we aspired to belong to.

In May 1973, I was promoted to lieutenant colonel. My immediate goal was to find a command. The centralized selection system for command of a few years later had not been initiated yet. In those years it was still a matter of making yourself available when an opening came up and hoping that the senior officers responsible for filling the command slot knew of you or would see your record and believe that you were the right person for the job. The chief of staff of the 3rd Armored Division, Colonel Sid Hazard, knew me from Vietnam and the G1 of that division, Lieutenant Colonel Jim Hattersley, was my old friend from our lieutenant days in Crailsheim in the 37th Armor. So, when the division's cavalry squadron commander was relieved for poor performance in June 1973, I was able to obtain the assignment as the new commander. The 3-12th Armored Cavalry, the 3rd Armored Division's cavalry squadron, was located in Büdingen, northwest of Frankfurt on the main road to Fulda. There could have been no better preparation for me for what lay ahead than the year I had just spent with General Collins.

13

THE SQUADRON

Büdingen, whose population was about 8,000 at the time, is a walled city nestled in the foothills of the Vogelsberg Mountain range. Though it was similar in size to the Crailsheim of my lieutenant days, it had been left largely untouched by World War II. This walled city dated back to the Middle Ages and had a real, live prince in residence, who still lived in his castle built in the fifteenth century. There were other castles spattered about the countryside, and the local aristocracy still rode to the hounds. Armstrong Barracks was a two-battalion *kaserne* built by the Germans in the years just before World War II, and it was located right on the edge of the newer area of the city that had expanded beyond the walls.

The *kaserne* was occupied by the 3rd Armored Division's cavalry squadron and its air defense artillery battalion, which were so-called division troops. That meant that the two units reported directly to division headquarters for all operational matters instead of to an intermediate brigade headquarters. The two units were also the most forward stationed units of the division because they would be the first to engage if an attack came across the interzonal border from the east. Only the "tripwire" armored cavalry regiments were stationed closer to the border than these two units. In the event of such a cross-border attack, the cavalry squadron would deploy in front of the division's heavy armor and mechanized infantry task forces to try to delay the enemy while reporting back on the routes and size of the enemy advance. The air defense artillery would also move forward to try to knock out the initial onslaught of enemy aircraft with its Chaparral missiles and Vulcan 20mm Gatling guns. The post commander for Armstrong Barracks was whoever happened to be the senior lieutenant colonel between the two unit commanders, but the commander of the 2nd Brigade, headquartered some twelve kilometers across the hills in Gelnhausen, commanded both units and the post for administrative functions and day-to-day activities. As always, such separated commands had their own set of challenges and resource issues.

The squadron headquarters building, a dark stone two-story building that dated from when the Germans built the *kaserne*, was set on a triangle of land that overlooked the junction where the road to the *kaserne* and two secondary roads from the smaller surrounding farm villages fed into the main road leading into the center of Büdingen. It was about a half-mile outside the gate to Armstrong Barracks. This separated headquarters building and the even further separated squadron commander's quarters across town belonged to the cavalry by tradition because previous to the advent of the divisional air defense artillery battalion, the other unit assigned to Armstrong Barracks had always been a tenant Corps Artillery unit. Therefore, the commander of the air defense artillery battalion lived in one of the field grade duplexes across the road, and its headquarters was located in a building on post in the center of its barracks area.

The space between the squadron headquarters building and the actual gates to Armstrong Barracks was bordered on one side by family housing apartment buildings, as was the space directly across one of the secondary roads that came into the intersection in front of the headquarters. The two sets of field grade duplexes were arranged on a cul de sac a little past the apartment buildings on the other side of that road. By tradition, though, we would live in the separate house that sat on a hill across town from the *kaserne* next to the Officer's Club. Those quarters had been the *Oberkommandant's* during World War II and had been confiscated when we occupied the area. We were to find that the quarters came complete with a bomb shelter behind an industrial strength blast door—as well as an enclosed sun porch that was rapidly separating from the house.

A mile or so out in the country, along one of those secondary farm roads, was the airfield, which was the center of activity for the squadron's air cavalry troop and its twenty-seven helicopters. The air cavalry troop commander position was a major's slot because of the additional responsibility that went with the job, whereas captains were the authorized grade for command of the ground cavalry troops. The air cavalry troop had a complement of forty-two officers and warrant officers, all rated aviators, which meant we had far more officers than the average battalion-size unit. The first time I flew with this unit, I came to understand that there was a world of difference between the professionalism of these aviators and the seat-of-the-pants approach that had been so common in Vietnam. On that first flight from Heidelberg to Büdingen and back on an unusually clear and bright German day, the warrant officer pilot practiced instrument landings at both ends.

I flew up to Gelnhausen to meet with my new brigade commander, Colonel Jim Aarestad, and spent the night at the visiting officers' quarters before being picked up by a vehicle from my new unit. At breakfast in the Officer's Club at Gelnhausen, I found out that there had been a disturbance in Büdingen during the previous night: a group of white soldiers and a group of black soldiers had gotten into a fight over who was to control the drug traffic in Armstrong Barracks. I wondered for a moment just what I had gotten myself into.

Since the previous commander had been relieved, there would be no change of command ceremony. The assumption of command formation would be very low key with no senior officers from either the brigade or the division in attendance. It was up to me to introduce myself, to take command, and to start putting things in order. For the time being I would be "batching it" in a single room in the small, one-story bachelor officer quarters nestled between the headquarters building and a family housing apartment unit while we arranged to move our family from Heidelberg after the school year ended. I had also left our car with the family, so I was going to be walking a lot unless I hitched a ride or used my command jeep.

The first order of business was to try to understand the circumstances that had resulted in the incident that had caused the relief of the previous commander. The incident had occurred while the squadron was on one of its cyclical training stints at Grafenwoehr. There had been a fight in the squadron commander's makeshift field camp office, of all things, involving three black soldiers, the command sergeant major, and the squadron commander. Apparently, at its conclusion, everybody had dusted themselves off and gone about their respective business. The brigade commander, Colonel Aarestad, happened on one of the enlisted participants wandering around with his boots unlaced and his trousers unbloused. He directed the soldier to get his uniform in order. The soldier responded that he could not because his arm was injured. Colonel Aarestad asked how he had injured it. The soldier responded that his squadron commander had hit him! An investigation followed, which resulted in the relief of the squadron commander.

I never found out all the details, but it was clear that the fight had started when the command sergeant major had put hands on one of the soldiers as they stood before the squadron commander in his makeshift office, and it was equally clear that, at a minimum, there was insufficient respect for the commander and his inherent authority to prevent the brawl that followed. The previous squadron commander was a couple of years ahead of me at the Military

Academy, had served in the same division as I had in Vietnam, and had also been on the faculty at the Military Academy when I was. He was a nice guy, if somewhat too laid back, but he had not served in a leadership role with troops since he had been a lieutenant on his initial assignment. This lack of progressive leadership experience may have been the root cause because after assessing the unit's condition and its level of morale and discipline, I could only conclude that he was unsure what it was he was building and even more unsure of how to get there.

I quickly found that neither noncommissioned officers nor officers would enter the barracks after 5 p.m., that there was a general lack of respect for the company grade officers, and that the noncommissioned officers had pretty much abdicated their leadership role and were just going through the motions of the daily routine. There were also some rumors of degrading initiation rites for newly arrived junior officers and of drunken formal occasions at the Officer's Club. While I could deal with the officer side of the equation, the noncommissioned officer problems led back to the command sergeant major. My first official act was to request a replacement. In short order I had a new senior noncommissioned officer, Command Sergeant Major Louis Gilmore, to help me build an effective unit. Though his experience was in airborne infantry rather than in armored cavalry, I could not have asked for a better senior noncommissioned officer leader. We set to work immediately.

While CSM Gilmore was starting to work with the noncommissioned officers, I discovered that I had an extra challenge on the officer side. The previous commander was still living in the commander's quarters across town. Though I never encountered him, his continued presence invited the captains and majors to consult with him after each of my commanders meetings. It appeared that our discussions on new directions were being vetted by my relieved predecessor. That was intolerable. Only a little less annoying was the fact that until he and his family moved on, I could not bring my family up, and I urgently needed my wife to help me with the social side of our new unit. The official reason for his not moving was that they were waiting for quarters to become available at his new assignment. Finally, I contacted a friend and classmate who held a senior staff position at his new assignment location and explained the situation and the need to get the previous commander out of our small community. A week later, he was gone!

Once my family was settled into our quarters, my wife and I began the process of getting to know the officers and their wives. We fell back initially on those courtesy calls of our early days in the service. I had the adjutant set up a roster that required calls on us at our house each Thursday night. We could get through a dozen to fifteen calls in an evening using the ten to fifteen minute rule—time enough to get to know names, have a light conversation and some light refreshment. The dress was informal (in those days, that still meant jacket and tie for the officer and appropriate afternoon dress or pants suit for the spouse) instead of the required blue uniform for the man and hat and gloves for the lady, but calling cards were required to be left so that we had a ready reference for names. That way, we quickly became familiar with our people: my wife was able to associate a wife with an officer and I was able to associate an officer with a wife. Bachelors, of course, were also included so that my wife got to know the names of those officers and associate the name with a face. It took a bit longer than usual because of the forty-two officers in our D Troop, but it was a good and relatively quick method of introducing ourselves to the squadron. We followed that by giving dinners on a Friday or Saturday night by troop, with D Troop, again, being split up into groups of four to six.

One Saturday night while I was working late in my office in the squadron headquarters before my family arrived, I was surprised to hear the unmistakable sound of a tracked vehicle moving down the road outside. Curious, I rushed out to find one of my M551

Sheridan vehicles disappearing in the direction of the back gate to the *kaserne*. I grabbed the duty driver, and we drove down to the motor pool. There I found a sergeant just locking up the Sheridan. A short conversation with a slightly tipsy sergeant disclosed that he had taken the Sheridan for a ride to a nearby *Volksfest* to show off his prowess to his German girlfriend. It was hard to count the number of policies and regulations that had been violated by that unauthorized drive. My disapproval of that kind of activity was dramatically announced by a reduction of one grade after a quickly convened summary court-martial. It was a start.

As it turned out, I probably should have been pleased that the Sheridan actually made it to the *Volksfest* and back without breaking down. If there ever was a vehicle that should never have reached production, it was this one. I can only be thankful that we never went into combat with it against enemy armor. The Sheridan had been introduced as the replacement for the M48A3 tank in the cavalry squadrons in Vietnam. It was designated as an armored airborne reconnaissance assault vehicle, and its name reflected its multiple design purposes, none of which it did well. It had light aluminum armor that was easily penetrated by machinegun fire or RPGs. My squadron in Vietnam had resisted accepting it in trade for our M48A3s based on what we had heard about these vulnerabilities. The forced replacement took place shortly after I departed from my unit in Vietnam, but the Sheridans shipped to Vietnam did not include the gun-launched missile system and its associated high technology guidance system. The main gun firing canister rounds and the machine guns worked well enough against infantry, but the light armor on the belly was vulnerable to mines.

By the time I joined my squadron in Büdingen, the Sheridan had been made standard for all of our cavalry squadrons. It had been designed light in order to swim and to be easily air transportable, but the problems with mines in Vietnam had caused additional belly armor to be added. With these thick steel plates welded to the bottom of the vehicle, it now weighed two tons more than its design weight. Though the modification made it more resistant to mine blasts, it also made it unable to swim and too heavy for an aircraft to transport more than one at a time. The added weight beyond the design weight also overburdened the transmission and the engine, leading to other maintenance problems. Given the problems that were encountered more recently with "up-armored" Humvees, it appears that the Army has recurrent problems with understanding the implications of tampering with design weight.

But the main cause of our maintenance problems was the gun launched missile system. The missile that was fired from the Sheridan was the Shillelagh anti-tank missile, and the gun tube had been sized accordingly. The result was a 152mm gun on a 15-ton vehicle. When the gun fired, the Sheridan lifted off the ground back to its third road wheel (about one third of the length of the vehicle came off the ground) and then slammed back down hard. Not only was that uncomfortable for the crew and made it very difficult to execute the burst-on-target technique used to ensure a second round hit in tank gunnery, but it wreaked havoc with the electronics with which the vehicle was loaded. It was still early in the electronics game and the transition to solid state was just beginning. The plug-in circuit boards were numerous, and every 152mm round fired would knock loose one of them, throwing some system out of kilter.

To further save weight and do away with the brass or steel shell cases that would normally litter the floor of a tank turret in combat, the 152mm ammunition was "caseless." The propellant charge was contained in a combustible cardboard shell that was supposed to burn up inside the chamber of the gun as the propellant that fired the projectile burned. This was another great concept that did not work because the remains of the cardboard shell of a fired round might still be smoldering in the chamber when the next round was loaded in. The results would not be good. To combat that problem, a scavenger system was added that used an air compressor to blow any remaining embers out of the chamber before the next round was loaded. The compressor system, of course, was vulnerable to frequent mechanical failure, which then would be cause to deadline the entire vehicle.

Eventually, it was determined that moisture could also affect the combustibility of the casing, so a neoprene boot was added to keep out moisture. That was in addition to the close-fitting, reusable fire-resistant nylon bag that protected the cardboard container against fire in the ammunition rack and had to be pulled off by an integral strap at the base of the bag as the loader loaded the round. Now the loader had to strip off the neoprene boot after pulling off the nylon bag as he gently pushed the round into the chamber. The combination of all these pieces made tank gunnery even more of a challenge than it normally might be, and keeping the system working was a nightmare.

But the worst design feature was an electrically driven breechblock that screwed in and out. Prior to this, all tank guns had a vertical mechanical breechblock that slid up as the round passed into the chamber and back down on recoil. That enabled a good gun crew to get two rounds off in six to eight seconds. In sixty seconds, a good tank crew could fire seventeen rounds while the Sheridan could fire only two because the Sheridan breechblock took eighteen seconds to unwind and eighteen seconds to rewind into the sealed firing position.

But the worst nightmare was caused by the combination of the breechblock being electronically driven and the shock of recoil that could dislodge the circuit boards that controlled the breechblock. It was possible on occasion for this combination to cause the breechblock to open on its own without the crew being able to stop it. The panic caused in the turret by seeing the breechblock unwind on its own after a misfire had been called had to be seen to be believed, and the ensuing panic was not an unreasonable reaction. A sister unit had suffered several fatal explosions as a result of the breechblock opening on its own after a misfire.

Automotively, the shock of recoil played havoc with all the engine fasteners, particularly since there was a lot of light aluminum used. The fan assembly would, for instance, come loose from the shock of recoil and eat its way back into the radiator, thus deadlining the vehicle for engine problems. To aggravate this maintenance problem, the scout sections that had been mounted in totally reliable modified armored personnel carriers in Vietnam were now mounted in Sheridans as well as the tank sections, which gave a total of six Sheridans to a platoon, eighteen to a troop, and fifty-four to the squadron. On a good day, we would have only two-thirds of them operational despite our best efforts. The Corps commander, who had been the program manager for the Sheridan program, lectured me every time he visited on how our poor maintenance practices were the cause of any problems with the vehicle, but those of us who had to use the Sheridan knew better.

Maintenance training quickly became a priority. Using the principles that General Collins had espoused, we set to work to schedule specific kinds of maintenance, always starting with a short training session conducted either by a mechanic or by the vehicle commander using the technical manuals that accompany every Army vehicle. That way we trained on the right way to maintain and then practiced it instead of having large blocks of time simply designated as "maintenance" during which each crew could do their own thing. Or not.

One of my immediate discoveries was that a number of my young lieutenants had absorbed too much about mission-type orders and too little about supervision. I would either find platoon leaders doing other chores when their platoons were doing maintenance or I would simply not find the platoon leader present when I walked through the platoons while they were doing maintenance. I kept being told by these platoon leaders that they believed in giving instructions and then leaving their men to do the job without them hovering. That theory may work with trained professionals, but it is doubtful for a platoon of soldiers, some of whom would rather be anywhere else. If you leave that group to their own devices in cold weather, you will find over half of them in the PX cafeteria in short order. My platoon leaders now had to learn to do their lesson-plan preparation some other time because it would not bode well for them if I found them absent from their platoon maintenance activities in the motor pool.

Shortly after I got settled in, my new executive officer arrived to fill the position that had been vacant when I took command. Major Don Williamson was a solid, detail-oriented officer who quickly became deeply involved in the maintenance and supply issues, leaving me time to devote to the many other areas that needed attention. He looked at the maintenance procedures in detail, he worked with the troop commanders on repair parts requisitions and on inventory issues so that there was renewed accountability for our equipment, and he provided assistance and counsel to the troop commanders on their supply and maintenance responsibilities. Without a good executive officer to share in the administrative burden, it would have taken a lot longer to get our unit moving in the right direction.

Major Williamson's presence allowed me to turn more of my attention to the discipline and morale issues that plagued the unit. There had been little apparent effort to identify and eliminate the serious slackers and drug abusers who were present in our unit. With CSM Gilmore as my main support in this area, we started motivating the noncommissioned officers to do their job in this regard. One of the reasons that they had stepped back from their traditional responsibilities was that there had been too little follow-through from their officers on troublemakers and problem soldiers that they had identified. The result was a belief that nothing they might do would be supported.

Many of these noncommissioned officers had a strong suspicion that the VOLAR programs were the reason for this situation. It appeared to them that the "power" was with the problem soldiers. So they stood back and watched when trouble developed, and they rarely entered the barracks after 5 p.m. Changing that attitude and getting them involved took time, and the first measure of success did not surface for almost six months. That measure was a knife fight in the mess hall that CSM Gilmore and I did not have to personally break up. The knife fight was reported to us after it was over by the noncommissioned officers who had stopped it and apprehended the major participants. Military justice followed quickly, and CSM Gilmore and I started to believe that our guidance, example, and noncommissioned officer classes were having the desired effect.

As the barracks became safer, the good soldiers started to take some responsibility for their living environment, and as the noncommissioned officers and troop officers increased their involvement in that environment, both the facility repair problems and the quality of life started to improve. The price in military justice, however, was high. In the two years that I would be in command, we would process thirty-four Chapter 10 (AR 635-200) eliminations from the service for unsuitability, two general courts-martial (one acquittal), three special courts-martial, and nine summary courts-martial (four acquittals). In addition, there was a steady flow of Article 15 non-judicial punishments for minor infractions and derelictions of duty, as well as reductions in grade for inefficiency.

The lack of discipline had still another effect: damage to our image in the community of Büdingen. When our soldiers acted inappropriately downtown in their off hours, it impacted our hosts, and that caused a need for apologies and, in some cases, restitution. The hurtful acts of indiscipline, typically under the influence of either alcohol or drugs, stretched from the thoughtless to the malicious. On the one end, our soldiers could not resist throwing empty beer cans at the prized black swans that swam in the pond in the park surrounding the Prince of Büdingen's castle. On the other end, soldiers under the influence of drugs or alcohol frequently made their way back to the barracks by walking over the tops of the cars that were parked bumper to bumper in front of the close-packed German homes (garages were a rarity because space was at a premium and street parking was the norm).

Despite the best efforts of our small military police detachment and our own nightly courtesy patrols, ending this kind of offensive behavior was a challenge. We had to identify those responsible and then take action that would fit the crime and serve as a warning to others. In the meantime, meetings to soothe feelings and to offer restitution took time away from other leadership responsibilities. Early on, I had been warned not to walk from town to the BOQ because it was unsafe. I made the walk anyhow as a statement, but I never encountered an "unsafe" situation. We did, however, have a very unsafe invasion by the German *Bereichspolizei* (state police) early one morning when, complete with submachine guns, they invaded the playground space in front of the family housing area searching for culprits from the night before who had apparently escaped into the playground in the dark.

Unfortunately, officers and their dependents could also be a cause for unhappy German-American relations on occasion. One morning I received a call from our Assistant Division Commander, a brigadier general, directing me to meet him at our airfield. I drove out and waited as his helicopter settled in, and he ducked out. Reaching my solitary jeep at the edge of the helipad, he asked if there was somewhere we could talk in private. Since we were not near anything but his idling helicopter and my jeep and driver, I suggested we simply walk a short distance away. The general then told me that our embassy in Bonn had received a complaint from the German government that the wife of one of my officers was having an affair with the Prince of Büdingen and that the family was concerned that she might get a portion of the estate. The complaint had been forwarded down through diplomatic channels to the division and now to me. The wife in question was, I knew, a horsewoman and had joined the local equestrian circle, which included the Prince, his family, and those with whom they intermingled socially. I asked if there were any evidence and was told that there was simply the allegation—and that I was to take care of the problem. With that, the general got back on his helicopter and flew off.

I was stunned! I could not envision asking the officer about his wife's relationship with the Prince for fear of destabilizing a marriage based on what might be a totally unfounded allegation. I was also annoyed that a simple allegation from a family member had blossomed into an official complaint that my superiors seemed to believe required immediate action. After some very discreet inquiries, I found that the officer's wife rode regularly, and frequently would be joined on morning rides by the Prince, who also rode almost every morning. Nobody had ever seen them together off their horses, other than in a crowded social venue after a foxhunt or at some other local equestrian event. I could only conclude that there were some interfamily jealousies at work, and I chose to drop the subject. I never heard from the general on the issue again. Apparently he had discharged his duty when he turned the problem over to me. Never a dull moment!

Even without German involvement, wives could cause a problem in our close-knit community. It was the era of hot pants, and the wife of one of my company officers had a white hot-pants suit that was her favorite wardrobe item. My wife and I first became aware of her preference in dress when she showed up with her captain husband for their official call at our quarters in what we came to understand was her trademark attire. The dress for these calls was "informal," which as mentioned previously meant shirt and tie for the man and an afternoon dress or pants suit for the woman. My wife restrained herself from commenting in this case about what was to us very poor taste.

As the weeks passed, we saw her walking through our small post on her way to the PX or post office in that outfit. Next, I started to get reports of obscene phone calls made to her quarters. While my wife and I were still puzzling over what to say or not to say to the officer or his lady, the unit moved off to Grafenwoehr for a scheduled training period. One night shortly after we had left, the wife called my wife to say that she was afraid that there was a "peeping tom" outside her first-floor apartment window. My wife promptly called the Rear Detachment Commander, a young captain who was my Adjutant in charge of squadron administration, and asked him to walk over to check the apartment. Shortly after my wife hung up, she received another phone call from the wife saying that she had heard somebody at her door and that she now had a loaded pistol with which to protect herself. My wife pictured the Adjutant getting shot while he tried to locate an alleged "peeping tom" who might have been attracted by the woman's attire to begin with. Fortunately, no "peeping tom" was found and no shots were fired, but it was a tense night for my wife.

A week or so later, my wife had to help deal with a senior noncommissioned officer's wife who had become unstable. She had some mental problems of which we were unaware. They surfaced when her husband went to the field. He had called home from Grafenwoehr to check on her, had been harangued by her about what she was going to do to the children and herself if he did not return from the field immediately, and he had then gone directly to his troop commander in a panic to return to Büdingen. The troop commander called the Rear Detachment Commander—who promptly called my wife for assistance. The captain, my wife, and the troop commander's wife went to her quarters, which was a rented apartment in one of the small neighboring farm communities. They tried to calm her, but my wife eventually had to arrange for transportation and accompany her to the psychiatric ward in the Frankfurt Army Hospital while the troop commander's wife stayed with the children. My wife vividly remembered for a long time what it was like to be locked in that psychiatric ward with the woman while she was being admitted. Obviously, command was a team effort. Since my wife was married to the squadron commander, it seemed to follow that she was the court of last resort when issues came up that stumped the young adjutant or needed a woman's point of view. She also was the means by which I found out about many of the family problems that inevitably arose.

The sergeant's wife was released shortly with a diagnosis that she was not mentally ill, but was a "manipulator" who would go to any lengths, including threatening violence to her children or a mental breakdown, to obtain her goals. In this case the goal had been to get her husband back from the field. The psychiatric assessment suggested immaturity as the cause and refused to recommend that the husband stay home or that either a compassionate transfer or hardship discharge were in order. The assessment also concluded that in view of the assessment that the sergeant must take the consequences of going AWOL to satisfy his wife. The sergeant, who had only recently arrived in the command, turned out to be a weak leader, but after some counseling we managed to avoid a repeat performance. In those days you could still discipline a soldier for failing to control his family, and the sergeant came to understand that I would use that tool if necessary.

Our troop officers' and senior noncommissioned officers' wives played a huge role in ensuring the welfare of the junior enlisted wives in their units. My wife had quickly identified the problem posed by these young wives with young children being alone in a foreign country when their husbands went to the field for extended training. By this time, approval to bring dependents to West Germany was no longer needed. Regardless of rank or quarters availability, a junior enlisted man could bring his dependents over if he could afford the airfare. Once there, the family was eligible for Army benefits and services. My wife and the troop wives organized a network to be sure that these young women were not left without the basics in their rented German apartments while their husbands were away. While the German landlords were particularly kind to these women, and even kept a lid on the rent as the dollar dropped in relation to the deutsche mark, the situation required something more.

Even though the families of junior enlisted troopers might not be authorized in the command, there was nothing to stop them from traveling from the States on their own and finding accommodations on the German economy. Once there, they had the benefit of the services provided by the Army: PX and commissary privileges, medical and dental services, and other support services located on post. Access to those services was, however, another problem.

There was a deep-seated fear among the married junior enlisted troopers that other soldiers would "hit on" their wives if they allowed them to go on post when they were not with them. So, they would drive the one secondhand car that the family owned to post when we went to the field and leave it parked there. That left the wife, many of them fresh out of small-town America and with no German language skills to speak of, to fend for herself and a young baby or two. She could not get to post to shop for basics; she could not get to the Post Office to pick up mail; and she could not pick up her allotment or the money sent back by her husband on payday. Even if she did somehow get the money, she could not easily exchange it for the much needed deutsche marks because she could not get to the exchange desk that we specifically set up on pay day to convert money for those who lived on the economy. Since changing the husband's attitude about allowing their wives to go on post without them was frankly beyond our abilities, the officers' and noncommissioned officers' wives network made sure there was transportation for the junior enlisted wives and that they did not run out of basics. They even made visits to ensure that all was well in the absence of the husbands.

When I became the Post Commander because of my seniority over a new Air Defense battalion commander, one of the improvements that we were most proud of later on in my tour was constructing and equipping a child care center. Our post was too small to warrant an official child care center, but Susan Bohannon, the wife of one of my aviator captains, made it her project. She found a suitable space in a company-size dining facility that was not in use because we had gone to consolidated dining facilities and she started from there. She recruited the volunteer labor and volunteer donations needed, and by dint of her hard work and perseverance, a community effort was put together to convert the old dining hall into a reputable child care center. I have a suspicion that it would not have passed inspection today, and there probably were a few regulations that got bent, but the end result, thanks largely to that young D Troop wife, Susan Bohannon, was a place where children could be cared for while their mothers did their shopping or just got to take a break from being the only parent while the men were away. Susan was prematurely taken from us by cancer some years later, but those early efforts were a memorial to her spirit so long as Armstrong Barracks continued as an active installation.

That facility rounded out the volunteer support system that the Army wives made happen. Thanks to them, we had a lending closet from which new arrivals could borrow the basics to set up housekeeping and an Army Community Service to provide various kinds of support to our families. All was directed, run, and supported by the volunteer hours of Army wives. The sense of community generated on those small, isolated posts a long way from home was something to behold and something that was much different than what might be encountered on large Stateside posts. That the social fabric of the Army was held together by the volunteer efforts of Army wives is an insufficiently recognized facet of the pre-working wife era. They raised families in isolated posts in a foreign country, put in volunteer hours during the day, and hosted dinner parties at night. When, in later years, society started to encourage outside careers for wives, the Army lost a huge part of that largely unrecognized, unpaid labor force that was the foundation for a good quality of life for military families no matter where they were stationed.

Somewhere in the middle of that first year, I was surprised to find a 1st Lieutenant asking to see me. He was not from our unit, and I was puzzled as to why he would be asking for an interview. It turned out that he was a recent West Point graduate and was assigned to the 11th Armored Cavalry Regiment on the border to the northeast of us, which was a plum assignment for any young lieutenant. He claimed that he had gotten off to a bad start with his troop commander and that he had permission to seek a transfer to start over. While I was not about to turn down the opportunity to add a Regular Army junior officer to my organization, I was a bit cautious as to why the 11th Armored Cavalry would be willing to release him. Units in Germany were still generally under strength in junior officers, particularly Regular Army ones, and it puzzled me why the regiment would be willing to let him go rather than simply transfer him to another of its three squadrons.

After I heard his story, I put in a call to the 11th Armored Cavalry's regimental commander and asked about the lieutenant. Sure enough, the colonel said that there had been some personality problems, and it appeared that it would be best for all concerned if the lieutenant transferred out of the regiment in order to provide a completely new environment in which he could get a fresh start without the rumors that would inevitably follow him within the regiment. That seemed to make sense, and I accepted him into the squadron without any qualms.

As the weeks passed, he appeared to settle in easily, but he also seemed not to be able to complete tasks as well as might be expected for his length of time in service. He would start a task with a bang, but his effort always seemed to peter out before the desired goals had been fully achieved. He did his job, but it was a listless performance that never sunk to the level of requiring counseling from me, but never quite lived up to expectations. I was aware of his lackluster performance, but not overly concerned since his troop commander would sort it out by mentoring him or in his efficiency report if mentoring failed.

Then two enlisted men asked to see me. They hesitantly told me that the lieutenant, their platoon leader, had propositioned them for sex! I called the lieutenant in for a conversation and told him of the allegations, which by then had been supported by sworn statements. He hemmed and hawed, neither admitting nor denying the allegations. I put in another call to the 11th Armored Cavalry's regimental commander, who had assured me that it was only a personality problem that had caused him to suggest a transfer for the lieutenant. I asked him if there was something more to the story that he had not told me, and he hesitantly admitted that there had been an allegation of predatory homosexual behavior and that he had actually drawn up charges, but had kept them in his desk drawer because he wanted to give the lieutenant a second chance in view of the fact that he was a second-generation West Pointer.

I promptly put through a phone call to the division commander and explained the situation to him. General Burton asked that I send the lieutenant down to division headquarters so that he could interview him. On his return, the lieutenant debriefed me and told me that everything had been cleared up. He had no sooner left my office than General Burton called me and told me an entirely different story. He had suggested that the lieutenant resign for the good of the service rather than face courts-martial proceedings for soliciting sexual acts from his subordinates. The lieutenant chose to resign.

Two things resulted from this incident. First, for the only time in my career I raised my voice in anger to a senior officer. The idea that the regimental commander had gifted me with an officer who posed a potential security risk (homosexuality was a reason for pulling a security clearance back then because of the very real risk of blackmail in those less tolerant days) and who had the potential to undermine the morale and discipline of my unit was almost beyond belief. I hung up after my tirade, and never heard another word from the colonel, who was promoted to major general some years later.

Second, I carried away from the incident a deepened concern for the presence of military members of any grade or of any sexual orientation who can become covert predators. The hierarchical nature of the military can lead to potential problems with any hidden inappropriate personal behaviors that are inimical to good order and discipline. It is simply too easy to use a position of authority to act out personal predilections with horrendous results. The Army's continuing problems with eliminating sexual harassment and sexual assaults, regardless of sexual orientation, is testimony to the difficulty of the challenge. Leaders must be especially alert and sensitive to possible covert personal-behavior issues that can result in a predator preying on a subordinate.

General Jonathan (Jack) Burton, the division commander who helped to resolve this very uncomfortable problem, was a superb division commander who, rumor had it, would not have been assigned to the 3rd Armored Division were it not for General Creighton Abrams becoming Chief of Staff of the Army. Burton was a true horse cavalryman who had been an equestrian from his college days on. Upon graduating from Michigan State University, he joined the Cavalry and was involved with the United States Olympic Equestrian Team both before and immediately after World War II. He had served in the Pacific Theater with the 1st Cavalry Division after it had been dismounted and had a distinguished record, but he had somehow wound up as the commander of the Army and Air Force Exchange System.

That was not usually a steppingstone to division command, but when General Abrams became Chief of Staff, there was a sudden change in projected assignments, and General Burton assumed command of the 3rd Armored Division. Once more, the pre-war cavalry associations bore fruit since both Abrams and Burton had served in the horse-mounted 1st Cavalry Division back then. There could not have been a better choice for a division commander for this particularly turbulent time. General Burton was calm and considered in his approach, and allowed subordinate commanders to do their job without interference so long as they performed well. The mistake that some made was to think that because General Burton rarely raised his voice or made direct demands, his soft-spoken guidance was not to be taken seriously. There was a heavy penalty for that mistake, but generally the division ran in a calm and purposeful way during his tenure.

On one of General Burton's many visits to the squadron at Grafenwoehr, he shared with a few of us the fruits of his experience in the South Pacific. We invited the General to join us for the noon meal on that occasion, a pleasantly warm, clear day, which is unusual in Germany. The nice weather had, however, brought out a swarm of insects on the barren ground that was the training area. They were beyond annoying, and it appeared that they would interfere seriously with our enjoyment of the food and the conversation as we sat on a sandy mound with our food trays. General Burton remarked that during his campaigns in the South Pacific, they had solved this kind of insect problem by tucking long stalks of grass into the elastic helmet bands that secured the camouflage cover to the helmet of that period. He quickly demonstrated what he meant, and we all followed his lead. Sure enough, the insects did not penetrate the screen of grass that hung down from the helmet just in front of our faces. It worked, and we had a pleasant meal and good conversation while the insects kept their distance—although the Lord only knows what passersby thought of the commanding general and several officers sitting in a group on the ground with their faces masked by those long stalks of grass. I've used the trick many times since, and it always works!

General Burton retired from division command to rejoin the Olympic equestrian world and to take up positions as an official, judge, technical delegate, and chief steward with both the United States Dressage Federation and the United States Eventing Association. He has since been inducted into the Hall of Fame for both organizations.

Slowly, the condition of the squadron and its effectiveness improved. Normal turnover brought in new officers and noncommissioned officers who had not been affected by the turmoil under the previous commander. As the Vietnam conflict staggered to a finish, more senior noncommissioned officers and officers became available and stabilized tours of three years once more became possible. Funding also improved, so facility repair started to take place. We had managed to eliminate or convict the majority of our troublemakers, and the elimination of the hardcore drug abusers had reduced that problem. In addition, intensive efforts on race relations had started to dispel some of the perceptions that had caused friction and even violence. More importantly, when incidents started, there were now noncommissioned officers and officers on the scene to take care of it. The improvement in these areas had enabled us to concentrate on maintenance and training to the degree that we performed well in our annual gunnery qualification and Army Training Tests. In short, the squadron was becoming a good unit—good enough that we did well when General Collins made one of his unannounced visits one morning. He found supervised training taking place in accordance with the training schedule and the general appearance of the facilities to be in good order.

Despite the overall improvement, an incident at Grafenwoehr while we were up there for our annual gunnery qualification

demonstrated just how volatile the situation could still be. B Troop
was having a stand-down day between ranges as we progressed
through the tank gunnery qualification cycle. Four troopers went to
the enlisted club that was operated by the Seventh Army Training
Center in a central location close to several of the field camps in
which units were billeted when not out training or shooting. After a
few beers, they approached a Puerto Rican soldier from an artillery
unit and asked about buying drugs.

The Puerto Rican soldier spoke little English and did not
understand them. They thought they were being put off and started
to harass the soldier, which brought the soldier's artillery friends
from his unit to his rescue. That potential incident was broken up
and the four soldiers departed, but they just could not stay away.
Back they went with reinforcements to satisfy their pride, and a
full-scale confrontation between the soldiers from the cavalry and
the artillery was in the offing. But thanks to some alert leaders, we
had seen the beginnings and were prepared. Officers and senior
noncommissioned officers moved in quickly and averted the
potential riot. A troop formation followed in which I read the riot
act to the entire troop, after which the four soldiers were charged
for disorderly conduct and restricted to our cantonment area to
keep them out of further trouble. The combination of race, alcohol,
and drugs can cause a problem if the chain of command is not ever
vigilant and willing to take prompt action.

Throughout this entire period, D Troop continued to turn
in an outstanding performance with a minimum of problems. A
number of factors combined to make that performance possible.
First, there were ample officers available to supervise the troop
with its complement of forty-two commissioned and warrant
officers. Second, the activities of the troop centered on the airfield
at some remove from the barracks area. Third, maintaining and
flying helicopters develops a special sense of responsibility because
there is no margin for error. The simplest of problems can lead to

disaster in flight. Avoiding those problems is a matter of pride. The D Troop enlisted personnel were by and large all skilled technical professionals who felt that responsibility and pride, which was tested every time an aircraft lifted off. In such an environment, there was little tolerance for drug abusers or troublemakers, and they were soon identified, isolated, and eliminated. The practical result was a consistent availability rate of around 70% for our helicopters and only two serious malfunctions, both hydraulic failures, during my tenure with the squadron. In both those cases, in one of which I was a passenger, the skill and strength of the pilot enabled him to land the aircraft without incident. The OH58 that I was a passenger in when its hydraulics failed as we were landing was a test of skill, but the AH1G Cobra that had a similar problem was a far greater challenge because of its configuration and weight.

In addition, I was gifted with two very professional, very strong aviator leaders during my time with the squadron. Major Bill Stubbs, a quietly competent leader, was in command when I arrived. He had steered the troop on a steady course of high performance through the turmoil that had immediately preceded my assumption of command. Major Stubbs was responsible for the airfield with all its multiple safety requirements as well as for the performance of the troop and the availability of its helicopters. Stubbs managed the airfield aspect of his responsibilities so well that the facility earned the highest rating possible in its periodic inspection. Given the breadth of Major Stubbs's responsibilities, the environment, and his limited resources, I recommended, and General Burton approved, the spot award of the Army Commendation Medal for his achievement.

Bill Stubbs was succeeded by Major Al Ferrea, a flamboyant leader with equally high standards. On occasion, I had to put some effort into maintaining amicable relations between Major Ferrea and our Assistant Division Commander, who was also a rated aviator. But because of the Major's penchant for challenging the general on aviation employment doctrine and philosophy, he had additional motivation to prove himself by running an outstanding operation. D Troop seemed to thrive under this new and different personality as well as it had under Major Stubbs.

Chief Warrant Officer Larry Morgan was a constant over the course of the tours of both commanders and was a role model for the more junior warrant officers. He was also the troop's instrument instructor, and it was his guidance that had motivated the pilot on my very first flight with the troop to practice instrument approaches on a perfectly clear day. Morgan was also responsible for instituting the training and certification that gave us much more flexibility with the weather than we might otherwise have had. Our valley was prone to inversions that pressed clouds down on us and resulted in limiting ceilings. Even if the minimum ceiling of 500 feet was available, the cloud cover could be 3,000 feet thick above it. The troop's response, thanks to Morgan's expertise, was for its instrument qualified pilots to go straight up through the ceiling into the cloud bank, at which point the pilot could pick up the navigation beacon that served our area and be acquired by the air traffic control system for our area. The aircraft could then continue with its mission whereas a less qualified pilot would not have been able to even lift off. Larry Morgan would later be the personal pilot for a succession of Commanders in Chief as a member of the elite flight detachment that supported the command section in Heidelberg.

In those days before the advent of an Aviation branch, commissioned aviators not only had to meet their flying-hour gates but also had to maintain branch qualification on the ground if they aspired to promotion. Major Ferrea, for instance, had already commanded a tank company when he came to the squadron. Those of my commissioned aviators who belonged to the Armor branch had the opportunity to accomplish both responsibilities in one tour, and it was not unusual for up to two of my ground troop commanders to be transfers from D Troop. That arrangement gave me the benefit of officers who were familiar with the squadron and gave the officers the opportunity to get their command time without changing stations. This cross training, though an extra burden for the officer involved, resulted in great cohesion and understanding between our ground and air elements in the field.

About the time that we started to be able to take a breath because the squadron was running well, the Air Defense Artillery battalion commander was reassigned, and I became the senior lieutenant colonel—and therefore, the post commander. Armstrong Barracks had a civilian population of about 800 family members to complement the 1,250 or so military members in the two units stationed there. There were also seventy-one civilian employees who operated the post exchange, snack bar, delicatessen, bowling alley, gymnasium, movie theater, service club, enlisted club, noncommissioned officer club, and the Officer's Club with its several guest rooms across town next to my family quarters. The family members lived in some 170 sets of government quarters and an uncounted number of apartments rented from German landlords in the surrounding communities. Problems or issues with any of these areas now came to me if the complaint could not be solved with the respective managers or landlords. I had one noncommissioned officer to help with this chore.

In addition, the close apartment living was a source of friction that caused complaints that ranged from laundry being taken out of the common, government-supplied dryers in the basements of the apartment buildings to a wife shooting her husband in the thigh (and that was not her true target) as a demonstration of her displeasure over his unfaithfulness. I quickly learned that family-member problems could not be put off; they had to be dealt with immediately no matter what else might be on my menu. I could only be thankful that I had been given a year to concentrate on my primary responsibility of leading a cavalry squadron.

My wife and I believed that the social side of our squadron was as important to the morale and cohesiveness of the unit as the other purely military aspects. Cohesiveness would grow, we believed, as the officers and their wives got to know each other and were able to enjoy social activities as a group. Our informal calls were followed by weekend dinners for groups of officers and their wives by troop. The forty-two officers in D Troop made the effort a little more challenging in terms of numbers of dinner parties, but the rewards were worth the work. Every six weeks or so there would also be a function at the Officer's Club with music and dancing for all the squadron officers, and a couple of times a year, there would be brigade-wide social events held at our club or at the larger club at the brigade headquarters post in Gelnhausen. But for the officers, the Dining-In, held twice a year, was a special highlight.

These were formal affairs patterned after the British regimental Dining-In or Formal Mess Night that combined humor, formal traditions, and entertainment. The British Army had a talent for staging these Formal Mess Nights that we could never approach. The best illustration of that is the story that was related to me during a visit to the Krupp mansion outside of Essen. *Der Huegel*, the home of the founders of the Krupp steel and arms conglomerate, had by then been turned into a museum. But shortly after the end of World War II, it had been used as the regimental mess for one of the regiments of the occupying British Army—the same Army whose first order of business was to put the Beck's Beer brewing plant back into operation. (The key-like "7" that still adorns the Beck's label is the insignia of the responsible 7th Division of the British Army.) The focal point of the ballroom is a wonderful carpet that covers all but the edges of the hardwood floor of the huge room and mirrors the frescos carved into the ceiling. On the evening in question, the regimental junior officers had already completed a race around the ballroom by swinging from the ceiling-to-floor draperies without touching the floor when a bet was made regarding crawling under the carpet for the considerable length of the ballroom. Legend has it that the first competitor did not even make it to the halfway point before he passed out and had to be rescued. The carpet was so closely woven that there was insufficient air underneath it to make the crawl possible.

Though we could not come near to this kind of flamboyance in Büdingen, there was a very real danger that if a Dining-In was not well orchestrated, it could turn into a "smoker." One of my predecessors had shown some pornographic movies and had the added bad judgment to have the sounds of the revelry piped over to the wives in the commander's quarters next door for the titillation of those present. That was certainly not our style, and I chose to concentrate on an aspect of the Dining-In that tends to be neglected. Among the other esprit-building purposes of a Dining-In is that of providing an occasion for junior officers to mix socially with senior officers in a non-duty environment. With that in mind, I tried to have general officers of the three- and four-star variety as my guests of honor for these events. In that way, junior officers could actually have an informal conversation in a social milieu with the 3rd Armored Division Commander, the V Corps Commander, the Deputy Commander in Chief (DCINC) for USAREUR, and the Commander in Chief (CINC) for USAREUR.

Though it was possible that some company grade officers might have a stilted question-and-answer conversation with the first two during official visits, and might answer questions for the DCINC on one of his unannounced visits, these were never the kinds of social interchange that were available at a Dining-In. In the normal course of events, of course, many company grade officers would never even see the CINC in person during an entire tour. But at a Dining-In, these officers could chat with this cast of characters over a drink and find out something about their experiences and outlooks during a normal conversation or the exchanges of stories. My assignments just previous to taking command made it easier for me to invite the DCINC or CINC, but generally speaking, such senior officers were delighted to participate in these events, which they found relaxing and reminiscent of their own junior-officer days.

My wife organized "Wining-Outs" for the ladies to run parallel with each Dining-In. Their formal dinner was held at a local German hotel ballroom and mimicked the ceremonies and traditions of the Dining-In. The wife of our guest of honor was asked to be their guest of honor, and she was usually eager to accept and to share memories of her early days as an Army wife.

There is a "rest of the story" to the Dining-In at which we were fortunate enough to have General Michael S. Davison, the CINC, as our guest of honor. He had been a lieutenant in the 12th Cavalry before World War II, and he and Mrs. Davison had been stationed on the border with Mexico when horse cavalry still patrolled that border. The invitation went out well in advance to General and Mrs. Davison, and we were delighted when both he and Mrs. Davison accepted the invitation to be the guests of honor for our twin functions. But then events beyond our little world shaped the day in a way that nobody could have foreseen.

Captain Alexander Haig had been a tactical officer during my cadet days at the Military Academy, and Colonel Davison had been his boss and our Tactical Officer Regimental Commander. Years later, General Haig was promoted over more senior general officers and designated as the next European Command (EUCOM) Commander and Supreme Allied Commander for Europe (SACEUR), the dual hatted NATO post that General Davison had been expected to fill when he left his position as CINC.

The promotion and assignment of General Haig effectively canceled that potential and caused General Davison to retire at the end of his tour as CINC. By complete happenstance, General Haig's assumption of command as the EUCOM commander in Stuttgart took place on the day of our Dining-In, and the Davison's flew to

Büdingen directly from that ceremony. One can only guess at the emotions that were hidden under the very calm surface that the couple presented to us, but I have always believed that it must have been a little bit of a relief to be able to come back to the unit where it had all started for them after the emotional turmoil wrought by a political decision that was totally beyond their control. Both guests of honor certainly seemed to enjoy themselves, and the respective formal assemblies thoroughly enjoyed the opportunity to hear stories of an earlier 12th Cavalry when a horse-drawn commissary wagon still delivered to her quarters the groceries that had been ordered by a lieutenant's wife.

Some seven months into my command another, even more senior general officer came to visit the Squadron. General Creighton Abrams, Chief of Staff of the Army, was on a tour of USAREUR. He had previously been both the Assistant Division Commander and the Division Commander of the 3rd Armored Division, so it was no surprise that he would visit the division. I had been steeped in the lore about General Abrams from the time of my first USAREUR assignment to the 37th Armor, which he had commanded during World War II, but I had never met him. The stories about him were legion, and his expertise as an Armor leader was legendary. On the day of his visit, he arrived on the CINC's two-car train at Gelnhausen, where the 2nd Brigade Commander, Colonel Jim Aarestad, met him. They drove the twelve kilometers to Büdingen in a sedan, and I met them outside my headquarters building to begin a tour of our training activities and our facilities. Apparently General Abrams, with a cold cigar clamped in his mouth, had been less than communicative on the drive over, so neither my brigade commander nor I knew quite what to expect.

We transferred to my command jeep and drove out to our local training area where we had set up a dry-run Table VIII on which our Sheridan crews were practicing. As we left the end of the road to enter the training area, my driver stopped to shift into four-wheel drive. Before we could start off again, General Abrams broke his silence to ask my driver how long he had been driving. Colonel Aarestad and I looked at each other from our perches on the radios in back of General Abrams, not quite knowing where the conversation was headed. My driver responded with the number of months that he had been driving for me, and the General remarked that he knew officers who had never learned to shift into four-wheel drive before they got into trouble.

Table VIII is the stressful final tank crew proficiency table where the tank or Sheridan crew must engage a series of targets for machine gun and main gun as they move down a prescribed route. Some targets are pop-ups, some are stationary, and some are moving. Our dry-run course was meant to give the crews preparation training for engaging these kinds of targets, getting the pre-firing actions down pat, and giving the appropriate fire commands that put any firing exercise into motion. At the end of each run, the crew was critiqued in a debriefing tent by a veteran senior noncommissioned officer who was an expert in gunnery and had ridden along as a "grader." As luck would have it, General Abrams entered the debriefing tent just as one of my weaker lieutenants was being debriefed on his very poor performance as the vehicle commander. Abrams came out of the tent shaking his head and asked me what I intended to do about the lieutenant. I told him that we would continue to train him and see what happened when we got to the real thing at Grafenwoehr in a couple of months.

On the way back to the *kaserne*, we passed by the Sonnenschein Batterie factory, which caused the General to ask me if the factory personnel were still raising Cain about our tracks leaving mud on the road in front of the factory. Our tracked vehicles picked up mud in the training area and dropped it on the asphalt road as they drove back to the post, which caused complaints every time it happened. I was surprised that General Abrams remembered the situation, and we kidded about the problem. General Abrams then remarked that when he had been the Assistant Division Commander he had always come forward when an alert was called and picked up a cavalry troop for security before moving further east into the Vogelsberg Mountains to set up his command post because he knew that was where the critical first battle would be fought in the event of a cross- border attack. None of my various Assistant Division Commanders had even indicated an interest in such tactical issues during my tenure. Rather, they had been more interested in buzzing the *kaserne* during alerts in a UH1 (Huey) helicopter to see how many lights had been left on after we departed for our dispersal area. I began to understand how the stories about "Patton's best tank commander" came to be.

The ice had been broken, and I think both Colonel Aarestad and I relaxed as we toured the track park, talked to maintenance sergeants about parts requisitions, and looked over the facility. Mrs. Abrams had accompanied the general, and the ladies had spent the morning entertaining her. She was a staunch supporter of the Girl Scouts, and my oldest daughter, Julie, was a girl scout. One of her projects was to compile an autograph book, and I had been charged with asking General Abrams to sign her book. So, as the visit wound down, I asked for his autograph for my daughter. He gladly gave it, and then he was gone.

Two months later, General Abrams was back in Europe escorting the Secretary of Defense, James Schlesinger. They came to Grafenwoehr and visited a range that I was running because Mr. Schlesinger wanted to fire a Sheridan. While the Secretary mounted a Sheridan to fire a round down range, General Abrams cornered me and asked me how that lieutenant was doing. Fortunately he had improved, and I could show the scores to support the assertion, but I was astounded that the Chief of Staff of the Army, without any aide to take notes, had been interested enough to follow up on his previous visit. As I escorted the General and the Secretary to a range where they could observe my D Troop helicopters going through their aerial gunnery paces, I listened to the two discuss national issues with the same ease that General Abrams had engaged a maintenance sergeant about the intricacies of the parts requisition system on his previous visit. His ability to switch between such widely disparate issues of our profession was truly amazing.

I do not know whether or not these two trips to a theater that he knew so well were in the manner of a farewell, but five months later, General Abrams was dead from cancer. His like may not come again.

And so, the months of command passed. We continued to improve, and General Burton's reward for that was to offer me an extension in command so that I would serve for two years as the squadron commander instead of the normal eighteen months. I was gratified and welcomed the challenge. New brigade and division commanders came in, stability of tours increased, problems decreased, and our effectiveness and skills continued to improve. We did even better in tank gunnery the next time around, and the Assistant Division Commander pointed out our range set-ups as the model to be emulated. With that high compliment a month before I left command, it was time to pack and say goodbye to the Squadron, Armstrong Barracks, Büdingen, and USAREUR. I had witnessed the low point of USAREUR at the beginning of this tour, five years before, and I had gotten to play a part in its resurgence. Ahead of me lay a short tour in the Office of the Deputy Chief of Staff for Personnel in Headquarters, Department of the Army, and then selection to attend the year-long course at the Industrial College of the Armed Forces in Washington, D.C.

14

RECALL AND *AUF WIEDERSEHEN*

My family and I would return to USAREUR one more time for another three-year tour. As I approached my graduation from the Industrial College of the Armed Forces two years after leaving Büdingen and cast around for an interesting assignment, a position became available as the Executive Officer to the Chief of Staff of USAREUR back in Heidelberg. My background suited me for the job, and we packed up the family for one more trip to Europe. At that point, our Siamese cats had made the trip to Europe and back more times than many people.

This time, we would remain in Heidelberg for the full tour, and my oldest daughter would graduate from the Department of Defense high school there. The graduation ceremony took place in the castle overlooking Heidelberg. My job was an administrative one, and I had little contact with soldiers. From my vantage point as Executive Officer to Major General Richard H. Groves, it was clear, however, that USAREUR had survived and risen from the ashes to the level of excellence that had been a matter of course back in 1960 when I had first been assigned to Crailsheim. Funding was better so the facilities were in good repair, tours were stabilized, German-American relations were solid, and training seemed to be generally effective.

This was the Army that would deploy to Desert Storm some years later and completely overawe the enemy with its tactics, equipment, and professionalism. Desert Storm came just as plans were being implemented to draw down USAREUR because the wall separating East and West had finally fallen of its own weight. The USAREUR units would redeploy from Kuwait and would start the drawdown that had been planned before Desert Storm. The remaining units would face arduous duty in Bosnia and Kosovo and would be deployed out of central Europe to the various hot spots in the Middle East and Afghanistan that would occupy the Army far more frequently than had ever been the case during the Cold War.

We had arrived in Germany when the signs of World War II were still very much in evidence, and we would leave for the last time after having seen prosperity take hold and *autobahns* built where there had been none or only two-lane asphalt roads. We would be long gone when the Berlin Wall was toppled in 1989, but we had been part of the force that was the deterrent that enabled the East German countermovement to develop and eventually topple that wall.

Most of the small *kasernes* have now been returned to the Germans, and many of them are abandoned or serve as refugee camps for the masses of third country nationals immigrating to Germany. The border is gone, the border outposts simply a memory, and the deutsche mark is gone. What remains are memories of duty well-performed on those small posts surrounded by farmland and small farm villages, of German friends from a time when the common threat was very real, and when our futures were intertwined in defense of the Western way of life.

When the first Desert Storm assault began, I had guessed at the timing, and I could visualize the marshalling of the tank and mechanized infantry columns. In my imagination, I could even smell the trademark diesel fumes rising above the columns as the 3rd Armored Division went forward across the line of departure into its last fight before it would be deactivated. The combat was mercifully short and the casualties mercifully few. I wrote to the commander of my old cavalry squadron to wish him well. He replied after the unit had returned to Büdingen. The squadron had suffered seventeen casualties during the entire period of combat; in Vietnam, we suffered seventeen casualties in a few hours or a day. May victory in combat always be achieved with so few casualties.

On Friday, January 17, 1992, the 3rd Armored Division cased its colors and marked the end of forty-eight years in Europe that began when it landed at Normandy. As the colors were cased, its last commander, then-Major General Jerry R. Rutherford, said, "The Cold War is over. Our mission is accomplished. It's time to go home." Those words applied equally well to USAREUR. Twenty-seven years later, however, that statement is under review because of the same common enemy that we faced during the Cold War.

A medal was belatedly struck for the participants in the Cold War. But for those of us who served in Germany during those years, the memories of raw wet mornings, mud, sudden alerts that you were never quite sure were only a practice, warm *gasthauses* with huge *schnitzels* and *pommes frites*, good German beer, kind German friends, the smell of honey wagons spreading their watery fertilizer over the fields, and the sense of having been part of something important are far more valuable than that strip of ribbon. *Kommen sie gut nach hause!*

Appendix

Ellie Mahler's retrospective on being an Army wife,
written for her 50th college reunion yearbook

Two weeks after graduation in June 1959, I walked down the aisle of the Old Cadet Chapel at West Point to marry my long-patient fiancé, Lt. Michael D. Mahler, U.S. Military Academy, Class of 1958. We flew to Kentucky the next day to look for a place to live since Fort Knox, his duty station, had no housing available for junior officers. My rose-colored glasses shattered quickly as reality struck. Our price range included made-over chicken coops with dirt floors—not exactly the honeymoon cottage I'd envisioned.

Thus began my twenty-three-year career as an Army wife, member of a unique sisterhood that worked together, played together, supported each other, and, yes, wept together too. The pay was non-existent, but the rewards were great. Our family spent ten-and-a-half years, on and off, in West Germany. We were there when the Wall went up, and we were there when bombs went off in the Heidelberg Army Headquarters where my husband worked. At age 36, I found myself the "Old Lady" of a cavalry squadron and the "Mayoress" of a two-battalion post in Büdingen, Germany. The men were gone on maneuvers for six weeks at a time—frequently. It fell to me to "mother-hen" the young, enlisted wives who had never been away from their hometown, much less the U.S. Suddenly, they were stranded in a foreign country, unable to speak the language, with no husband, little money, no transportation, and perhaps a sick baby. We ran a day care, a lending closet, a thrift shop, volunteered at the Red Cross and at the schools, held benefits, and socialized at formal and informal dinners that we hosted. I weathered Vietnam and the Tet Offensive, and I was grateful when my soldier returned home in one piece.

We raised two lovely, successful daughters, and they have gifted us with five delightful grandchildren. Are we blessed? You bet!